ICE AND RAINBOWS

A Wisconsin Girl's Memoir
of Iceland

———◇———

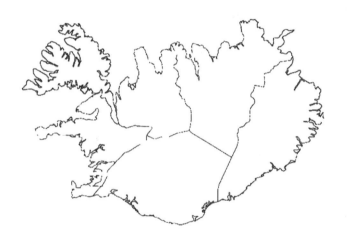

Paula A. White

5-25-23

Dear Starker,
    To my one and only
    brother, love you so!
Happy Reading,
    your little sis'
        Paula

Paula White, Bifröst class photograph, 1978.

*This book is dedicated to my parents Betty and Keith
and my Icelandic host parents Ásta and Jón.
You've inspired me, taught me, and I love you.*

ACKNOWLEDGMENTS

To my parents, Betty and Keith White, for allowing their sixteen-year-old daughter to live in Iceland, planting my interest in travel and languages, and raising me to be brave and never give up. To my Icelandic parents and host family for taking me in and opening their hearts to me. My deepest gratitude goes to them for their love and endearment during my school year in Iceland and beyond. I am indebted to the Rotary Club of Green Bay and Borgarnes. Without them, this experience would not have been possible. To my family for their encouragement and for enduring the lengthy process for this book to come to fruition. To my sister, Robin White, and my dad, Keith White, for reviewing a draft of my very first chapter and inspiring me to continue. To Carolyn Schott, my editor, for her invaluable recommendations. To my friends who have offered endearing advice and support, I thank you from the bottom of my heart. To my husband Danny, there aren't words enough to thank you for your tireless editing, for enduring countless hours of reminiscing and contemplating the meaning of this experience, and for all the adventures we have yet to discover together.

While all the stories in this book are true, some names and identifying details have been changed to protect the privacy of the people involved. I apologize in advance for anything or anyone I might have misrepresented. This is my Icelandic story, the way I remember it.

PREFACE

When I went to study in Iceland in 1977, I was desperate to escape the routineness of high school in Green Bay, Wisconsin. I may not have been a typical high school student. I used the evenings and weekends to study and write long, researched papers for my classes, and practice piano, tap, ballet, and folk dance. Following my first trip to Europe with my family in the summer of 1976, I knew that foreign travel was for me. One afternoon at my high school, I heard an announcement over the loudspeaker that the Green Bay Rotary Club had openings for two exchange students for the upcoming school year: one in Mexico and one in Iceland. I ran home to check the atlas to see where Iceland was located and the encyclopedia to see what language Icelanders spoke.

In my interview, the Rotarians asked which country I preferred. I knew my chances of being selected would be greater if I chose Iceland. What high school student in their right mind would want to go to this unknown, cold island of ice and spewing volcanos?

A few days later, I jumped up and down excitedly when I received the acceptance call. Meanwhile, my mom was weeping in distress. I had no idea what being an exchange student entailed. Now, I can't imagine my young life without this Icelandic experience. Iceland's unique language, culture, geography, and pristine beauty have forever shaped my heart and personality.

Filling five journals in tiny handwriting during my stay in Iceland was time-consuming but also comforting when I lacked close friends. Reviewing the journals allowed me to recollect specific details of conversations and experiences. I had to laugh at how detailed I recorded certain things, such as what I ate for every meal and what I wore each day. Pulling out the stories to share was like whittling away at large pieces of wood. It's taken me over forty years to recount this journey while I finished graduate school, got married, worked several jobs, and traveled the world before finding the opportunity to share these deeply felt memories.

The subsequent chapters follow a teenager's adventures chasing ice and rainbows in a time when Icelanders had rarely witnessed a sixteen-year-old foreigner attempt their language or culture. This is not a travelogue about where to eat, where to stay, or what to see. I have no intention of critiquing the Icelandic people or culture. This was my experience, through my eyes, including the good times, the funny adventures, the challenges, and the everyday events. I try to maintain the integrity of my journals to reflect what was on the mind of a sixteen-year-old at the time, including diet, dating, fitting in with peers, and the various predicaments I got caught in.

Many of the insights presented in these chapters emerged during the course of writing the book and reflecting on what had transpired during my exchange. Some of these experiences could have happened to a sixteen-year-old living anywhere. What occurred when I lived in Iceland in the late 1970s does not necessarily reflect what life is like in the country today. As I wrote this memoir, I was struck by how little foreigners knew about the country when I lived there, compared to what a popular tourist destination Iceland has become nowadays.

Until I could understand Icelandic, I lived without knowing where I was going, what I was going there for, how long I'd be there, who would be there, or how I'd get home. Even when I learned more Icelandic, I remained in the dark about many details of my activities, like attending a boarding school, climbing a glacier, a trip to the hospital, and taking a cargo ship around the circumference of the country.

When I was awarded the scholarship, Rotary International informed me that I would have three host families during my stay. Being hosted by three different families would provide an opportunity to become acquainted with a wide variety of people, customs, and family life. It was also a method to divide the labor and enable more families to enjoy hosting an exchange student. This did not work out as planned. My first family became my only host family. I did not have a host family when I was sent to boarding school for the second half of the school year. While I attended the boarding school, my original host parents, Ásta and Jón, invited me to their home in Borgarnes for several weekends and holidays. I was also lucky to get well acquainted with their extended family. Their daughter Svandís and their oldest son Björn, who each had spouses and young kids of their own, opened their homes to me and showered me with such endearment that I loved them right back. In a letter, Ásta and Jón's younger son Árni wrote to me from Illinois, where he was living as an exchange student. He said,

> *I know that you are not alone when you stay with my family*
> *when you have won their friendship like you have done.*
> *Because they have written to me that they like you very*
> *much. I am getting a little bit afraid that they don't want me*
> *back. But I will be back anyway, even if they want to keep*
> *you* (personal correspondence, November 15, 1977).

Iceland is often referred to as the land of ice and fire. I use the words ice and rainbows in this book as metaphors. First, the ice as the bountiful glaciers and icy landscapes, combined with Icelanders' reputation for having an icy exterior with a warm, friendly inner personality. Second, the colorful rainbows in Iceland that often follow rainy weather refer to the joy of overcoming challenges, learning the language, and fitting in.

Frank McCourt, in an interview about his memoir *Angela's Ashes,* put into words what best explains why I had to write this memoir of Iceland:

It helped me to face my past, to achieve that freedom…
The best thing is to have done it. It had been gnawing at me
for 30 years (in Boetig, 1999).

A note about the Icelandic alphabet: Many Icelandic words, names, and places appear in the book using the Icelandic alphabet. Some non-English letters may be unfamiliar to the reader. I intentionally use the original Icelandic spelling to allow the reader a first-hand look at the language. To avoid interfering with the flow of the text, the unfamiliar vowels (á, é, í, ó, ú, ý, æ, and ö) can be read roughly similar to English. The two letters, ð and þ, can each be read as an English "th".

FALL/HAUST 1977

CHAPTER 1

Breaking The Ice

"Bíta á jaxlinn."
Literal meaning: Bite the molar.
Intended meaning: When life gets tough, just push ahead.

My head bolts upward as I feel cold wetness on my forehead. Squinting, all I can see is a blurry image of a small dark room. A fuzzy silhouette dabs something on my forehead, making me feel trapped. I try to sit up to get out of here, wherever "here" is. A white-clad woman pushes my head back down. She rolls up my sleeve and squeezes my arm before dabbing my forehead with a cold compress.

I drift in and out of consciousness until I hear a deep male voice saying, You know, you're in the hospital. No, I didn't know that, not until now. I'm baffled by where I am and angry that they won't let me sit up. Even if they would, I don't have the strength to move or the energy to express any words. I struggle with my brain, feeling as though it has somehow floated outside of my body. All I feel is the cold compress and the urge to sit up. I have no sense of place, who I am, or why I'm here. Slowly, I glance out the window and obtain a remembrance that I'm in Iceland. Am I in Borgarnes or Reykjavík? Is it morning or night? All I see is pitch darkness. Because of Iceland's long, dark winter days, it could be any time of day.

The white-clad woman keeps asking, Are you still dizzy? I'm not sure if she's speaking in English, only I understand her. I search for clues to figure out my circumstances. Digging deep inside my brain, I gradually remember my first glimpse of the rugged Icelandic landscape spotted with craters and vast expanses of large brown boulders.

But how did I come to be in Iceland? I'm starting to recall the details. It's September 10, 1977, I'm sixteen, and I've just flown into Iceland's International Airport in Keflavík to spend a school year as a Rotary International exchange student. Leaving my home, family, and friends in Green Bay, Wisconsin, my heart pounds fast as I meet my host family. I don't know any Icelandic, and my host parents don't know English. What was I thinking to come here? What will it be like to learn the closest language to Old Norse?

Jón (pronounced "Yōn"), my host father, has an honest and caring face. He manages the electric company in Borgarnes, a farming town with 1,400 residents. I'm disappointed to learn that Borgarnes is so rural, located 75 miles north of Reykjavík, Iceland's capital and largest city. I meet my host mother, Ásta, who has a warm and loving face. Jón is seven years older than Ásta and fourteen years older than my parents. My host parents have three kids. The two oldest are each married with kids of their own, giving Ásta and Jón six grandchildren.

A short drive west of Reykjavík, we arrive at Ásta and Jón's daughter Svandís' apartment in Seltjarnarnes where she lives with her husband Birgir (pronounced "Beergeer") and their four kids, Ásta Margrét (fourteen), Vigfus (eleven), Birgir Jón (six), and Linda Björg (four). When I greet the family, I see that except for my braces, my pale complexion and light-colored hair will fit perfectly with the Icelandic norm displayed by Svandís, Birgir, and the kids. It's a relief to discover that both Birgir and Svandís speak English well.

Because of the jet lag, Svandís suggests that I nap before lunch and shows me to her oldest daughter, Ásta Margrét's bedroom. At fourteen, Ásta Margrét is tall for her age. She is stunning with her champagne blonde hair and sparkling blue eyes.

After a brief nap, we have lunch at the small circular table in the kitchen. I've never had lobster served as bite-sized pieces in a cream sauce before. It goes well with the cheddar cheese I brought as a gift from Wisconsin and their dark Icelandic rye bread. The strong sulfur smell from the hot tap water makes me crinkle my nose until I remember reading that Reykjavík uses geothermal water to heat its buildings and homes.

To get to Borgarnes, Jón and Ásta take me on the two-and-a-half-hour drive past bare lava mountains. When I see the sign *Velkomin til Borgarness*, I consider this a personal welcome. Ásta shows me to my room in their two-story, three-bedroom house overlooking the stark brown-colored Borgarnes fjord.

I'm borrowing the bedroom from their son, Árni, who's studying in Antioch, Illinois, this year. It is spacious, with a purple and black plaid sofa bed, a desk, and a stereo system filled with Árni's rock-and-roll albums. Looking around the house, I take in the living room with its antique furniture and dark brown curtains. I feel a moment of homesickness for the easy casualness of the messy newspaper piles next to the fireplace at home in Wisconsin.

Svandís, Birgir, and their kids also make the drive from Reykjavík to welcome me to Borgarnes. Having settled into my room, I join Svandís and Birgir on the back veranda to view the fjord hugging the town. The primary color outside is golden brown, unlike Wisconsin's flowing green landscape, at least in spring, summer, and fall. Except for the colorful exteriors of the nearby houses, the roads are dark lava brown, with treeless, blue-brown mountain tops peering over the fjord. I get a twinge of loneliness looking at this austere landscape and hearing the foreign Icelandic words I'm working hard to grasp.

When we say goodnight, both Ásta and Jón reach for me and kiss me right on the lips. Aside from never having been kissed on the lips before, I'm not sure how well I must know the other person to engage in this custom. In my attempt to absorb the culture of my new adopted country, this is just one of the customs I'll have to learn to accept.

Ásta has prepared the pull-out sofa bed in my bedroom with a fluffy down comforter covered with a white duvet and a large down bed pillow topped by a tiny one in the middle. I study the arrangement since I need to know how to tuck the down comforter, sheets, and pillows inside the couch each morning and then re-dress it at night.

Although everything in Borgarnes is foreign to me, my surroundings, the time zone, and the sofa bed with an extra small pillow in the center of the mattress, I sleep soundly. In the morning, I step out the front door and notice that the air feels different. Being 3,000 miles from my family, in another country with a different language and culture, gives me a strange feeling unlike anything I've ever known. Exploring this new foreign town and learning my new language has me giddy with anticipation.

In the kitchen, I munch on a bowl of strange breakfast cereal. I examine the box to discover it comes from Finland. The texture is much chewier than I expected, and the flavor is less sweet, making me wish I had poured a smaller amount. Birgir tells me that much of the food here is imported from other countries, making it quite expensive. The orange juice tastes like it's made from instant Tang crystals, as used on John Glenn's space mission. I wonder if it tastes that way because of the moon-like landscape here.

Jón drives Birgir, Svandís, and me a short distance to the community garden plot, where we gather a bucket of potatoes for dinner. It's funny to compare the tiny size of these potatoes to the mountain of vegetables my dad grows at home in Wisconsin. Birgir says that the coming frost makes it necessary to gather potatoes when they're this tiny.

The more I learn about Borgarnes, the more I compare it to Green Bay. I thought Iceland would be even colder than Wisconsin's winters. However, I've been told Iceland isn't as cold as its name suggests. Iceland's average winter temperature of 40 degrees Fahrenheit is practically short-sleeve weather in Wisconsin. Except I am already noticing a constant wind chill.

My fear of not being able to communicate is coming to fruition. Birgir and Svandís must return to Reykjavík. This means the end of any normal conversation since my host parents don't speak English. I thought Jón knew some English from the letter he wrote me before coming here. Now I learn that Birgir wrote the letter on Jón's behalf.

We say our goodbyes, *Bless, bless*. The words sound like English, only they're a shortened version of the more formal Icelandic phrase, *Komdu sæll og blessaður*, meaning "come happy and blessed." Without English speakers in the house, I'll need to rely on sign language and a tiny English-Icelandic dictionary to communicate with Ásta and Jón.

It's clear if I'm to do any socializing, I must learn Icelandic as quickly as possible. Studying the language has become my primary objective, working with the dictionary, developing flash cards, and trying to expand my, up until now, nonexistent Icelandic vocabulary.

It helps when Björn comes over for breakfast, as he knows some English and can help with translation. Björn is Ásta and Jón's oldest son and goes by the nickname Bubbi, pronounced *Buh-pi* with a long "u." Bubbi and his wife Anna live in a duplex about a ten-minute walk away with their two kids, Ásta Björk (nine) and Jón Bjarni (seven). Bubbi is tall and thin, with a long, narrow face, and a deep voice. His deep brown eyes, brown curly hair, and darker complexion prove that not all Icelanders are blonde-haired and blue-eyed. He works as an electrician in Borgarnes and the surrounding area. Anna, his wife, works as a secretary and accountant at the Electric Company, which means Jón (her father-in-law) is her boss. The Borgarnes Electric Company seems to be run entirely by my new host family.

Jón and Bubbi capture my full attention during breakfast when they repeatedly fill their cups with tea and cover several slices of toast with a selection of herring, sliced lamb, and cucumber and tomato slices. After Jón and Bubbi leave for work, Ásta and I walk the two blocks to the fish market. The market is located inside the grocery store on the small, modest main street. On this windy, rainy day, the air smells cold. I'm glad to have worn my hat and ski jacket. I'm learning this nasty windchill is typical for September and will be for the months ahead.

The fish are displayed whole and uncleaned in large baskets filled with ice. I haven't seen a market like this in Green Bay where we primarily buy frozen or smoked fish. After a thorough inspection, Ásta selects three large fish, which the clerk slices and weighs. The salesclerk's daughter cleans the fish while she talks to Ásta. Another woman enters the market, and Ásta introduces me to her. The woman speaks some English and says, It's good you're staying in Borgarnes instead of Reykjavík since you'll like Borgarnes better. She tells me how wonderful it is to live in Iceland.

I'm starting to get hungry, making me realize the house has a persistent fishy smell. Back home, I haven't been a huge fish fan, except here, it tastes delicious, so I don't mind the odor. Ásta prepares the fish from the market, a tender white fish without a fishy taste. Fortunately, I like it since this is to become my main diet here. Fishing is the primary industry in Iceland, compared to Wisconsin, where cows and corn fields dot the landscape. Ásta serves the fish with the tiny potatoes we harvested from the garden the day before, and we drink tall, cold glasses of milk.

A pleasing aroma comes into my room, waking me early in the morning. I find Ásta in the kitchen making *kleinur*, a new Icelandic word, and food for me. Talking about cooking and baking is a convenient connection with Ásta and is helping to expand my Icelandic vocabulary. It turns out that *kleinur* are a type of twisted fried dough, like donuts without holes. The *kleinur* aren't quite done, so we relax on the brown grass in the backyard. Ásta has me fooled that she's found a four-leaf clover until I see that she's carefully attached the fourth leaf. She places her four-leaf clover creation in a plastic box for me to save for good luck.

While I'm in the perfect situation to get total exposure to Icelandic because Ásta and Jón speak no English, I'm frustrated at how slowly my Icelandic is progressing. I now have two books to help me learn the language. One is a small handbook with tiny print and detailed grammar explanations beyond my practical ability at this early stage. The other is a teach-yourself handbook that's more my style, and I'm drilling daily. When I met their son, Árni (nicknamed Addi), in Green Bay before coming to Iceland, he predicted I would never learn Icelandic. My goal is to prove him wrong.

Anna (Bubbi's wife) comes over with her kids, Ásta Björk and Jón Bjarni. She speaks in a friendly voice, asking if I would like to go for a drive in the countryside. Luckily, she knows quite a bit of English. We collect potatoes from the garden plot, and then pass several farms and stop to get a closer look at the sure-footed Icelandic horses I've read about. Next, we visit a quaint little church in a township called Borg á Mýrum, due west of Borgarnes.

As we drive along, Jón Bjarni is chewing five pieces of Juicy Fruit gum at a time. He's pulling the massive wad of gum in and out of his mouth directly behind me. Just as I feared, the gum falls out of his mouth and ends up stuck in my hair. Anna examines the sticky, gummy knot. She frowns and tells me, We'll have to cut it out.

We stop at a nearby farmhouse. Anna explains our predicament to the woman and her daughter. Eager to assist, they have me sit in a chair and begin to operate. They use a multi-purpose household oil, with a deep, penetrating smell, to dab on the now firmly packed wad of gum in my hair. Several long minutes of concentrated rubbing and pulling finally does the trick, and they get the gum out. I grimace as I feel what remains is an ugly cowlick for me to keep as a cheap souvenir. This is one way to meet the neighbors.

Anna will give me a ride to Reykjavík to attend Ásta and Jón's godson's wedding. I've only been to a few weddings in Wisconsin and am excited at the prospect of attending a wedding in Iceland. We stop at a traditional Icelandic round-up on the way out of town. I snap several close-up photos of the fluffy black and white sheep. A drunken man staggers up to me and shouts something incomprehensible in Icelandic. Anna warns him off and explains how common it is for people to get drunk at these events.

Continuing along the rough and gravelly road, we hear a loud popping noise and discover Anna's Volvo has a flat tire. It's ferociously windy as Anna changes the tire. She tells me we can take the half-hour ferry the rest of the way from Akranes to Reykjavík. As we wait for the ferry, Anna and I snack on shrimp sandwiches from the kiosk while the kids eat Icelandic hot dogs called *pylsur*. The hot dogs here are much longer and skinnier than those back home, and they're made of lamb with a bit of pork and beef.

I've ridden on a ferry once before, from Manitowoc, Wisconsin, across Lake Michigan to Ludington. I was eleven then, and the only snack we could find to divert our attention from getting seasick was M & M's. With that in mind, on board the Akranes ferry, I concentrate on chewing gum to avoid seasickness. As we approach Reykjavík's harbor, we climb up to the top deck to see the brightly colored red, blue, yellow, green, and orange rooftops that the city is known for.

Now that I've been living in rural Borgarnes for a week, it's strange to hear the hustle and bustle of city traffic. Iceland's capital city, Reykjavík, is home to 100,000 people, or half the country's population. Anna drives us to her parents' house, and I'm introduced to her mom and dad, her sister, her sister's fiancé, and her sister's six-month-old baby. It's common for couples in Iceland to have babies before they get married. From what Anna tells me, the social stigma of having an out-of-wedlock baby isn't as much as in the United States. Although more babies are born to unmarried women in Iceland, it's common for mothers to eventually marry their child's father.

At breakfast, Anna hands me a tube of caviar to spread on my toast. I smile as this is my first-time trying caviar out of a tube. I doubt anyone in Wisconsin will be having this for breakfast. My hands and ears are numb from a brief walk outside with Anna's kids. As I read the Icelandic *Morgunblaðið* newspaper, I need to consult the dictionary to translate nearly every word.

I pack my suitcase to move from Anna's parents' house to Svandís and Birgir's apartment and unload my books. Now that I'm studying from two Icelandic language books, my host family is under the impression that I'll soon be fluent in Icelandic. I enjoyed studying Spanish in Green Bay, which has made me eager to learn another language. However, I'm finding Icelandic pronunciation and grammar are more confusing and complicated than Spanish and English. Anna warns me, I think you'll have a tough time in school, knowing no Icelandic. I'm sure she's right.

Ásta and Jón arrive from Borgarnes to prepare for the wedding. During lunch, I have several mishaps. First, I fail to take the peelings off my potatoes, which turns out to be a big mistake, and the kids laugh. Second, I almost serve myself from the cat's bowl of fish. Why is it on the table, I wonder, only it's not polite to ask. In addition, I use the wrong sauce for the fish, making me feel like a dumb foreign student. I just smile in response to their laughter to hide the awkwardness I'm feeling.

Ásta irons my red-and-white-checkered and lace-adorned floor-length dress and raves about how pretty it is. Seeing me in my fancy dress, Birgir teases me, Are you the bride? Svandís admires my red and white flowered jewelry that coordinates with my long dress. I feel very grown-up when Jón asks me to help him with his cuff links.

When we reach the front doorstep of the bride's house, a man directs us up a steep stairway. I feel out of place as I notice my dress is more formal than the others. Also, I'm the only person here who doesn't know Icelandic. I try to make sense of what the wedding hosts and guests are saying from the few Icelandic words I know. Despite my best efforts, I can't discern much. All I can do is pay close attention to people's expressions, hand motions, and tone of voice.

I'm offered coffee, No thanks. I accept a Coke instead and take small sips to make it last and to help pass the time. An hour later, Ásta points to show that I'm to go with a girl named Ása. I'm unsure where we're going, but I follow Ásta's instructions.

I discover that we're headed to the church. Ása and her friend are busy greeting guests with Icelandic kisses while I stand alone, wondering what to do. I follow them down the aisle and see Jón and the groom standing at the altar. All the women sit on the left and all the men on the right. The entire church is silent while Ása and her friends talk rapidly in muffled whispers.

Following a long ceremony of incomprehensible words, we move outside to the front of the church. Each wedding guest congratulates the bride and groom. I'm not sure what to say. When it's my turn, instead of an Icelandic kiss, I kiss each of them on the cheek. Without any originality, I say, *Congratulations*, in English. The bride replies graciously, *Thank you*, to me, also in English. I miss the rice-throwing and the decorated wedding car, and no one honks their horns on the drive to the wedding reception.

The reception is at the bride's parents' house, a stately structure built out of heavy cement to withstand the harsh weather. The adults stand talking in the ornately decorated living room. The heavy cigarette smoke is irritating my eyes. Looking at Ásta and Jón, I realize that leaving is not possible.

Another hour passes with no one to talk to until I join the line for the wedding buffet. Plates of ham, chicken, smoked mutton, salmon, shrimp, salads, and fruits adorn the dining room table. My eyes nearly pop out when I see how high the guests heap their plates. A man beside me explains in English, It's okay to return for seconds. Since a friend of Anna's warned me that exchange students tend to gain weight, I have no intention of falling into that trap and reply, No thanks.

Once we've said our goodbyes and head out the door, I sing in a whisper to myself to make up for hours without conversation. As soon as we return to the apartment, Birgir asks, How was the wedding? Fine, I say. I don't think it's polite to admit how difficult it was to sit for hours in a crowd without anyone to talk to. Going to an Icelandic wedding isn't that fun if you can't speak to anyone.

Ásta and Jón plan to drive home to Borgarnes this evening. Jón asks me if I'd like to remain in Reykjavík. I'm happy to stay because I'm craving the liveliness of Svandís' family. Svandís returns from the store with chocolate mint ice cream. I'm fascinated to watch her slice servings out of the box with a knife rather than scoop it out like we would at home. Reading the ice cream label and discussing the Icelandic words on the box is more interesting than trying to study Icelandic grammar out of the book.

Even easier is to watch the end of a Walter Matthau movie in English on TV and then help Ásta Margrét with her English homework. Birgir lectures us in English. You should help each other with your language studies. I'll take you downtown if you work together for an hour tomorrow.

I don't need a bribe to practice Icelandic. I'm already motivated enough by my need for survival. As I continue practicing the exercises in my Icelandic grammar book, I feel better about the pace at which I'm learning new vocabulary words. I'm even beginning to ask questions and use complete sentences in Icelandic. I say, *góða nott* (good night) to Ásta Margrét, and we smile at each other when she says *good night* to me in English.

I'm reminded of how tiny the country is when we run into Svandís' mother-in-law at the shopping center on the way to buy a birthday gift for her. It isn't possible to go out in Reykjavík or Borgarnes without bumping into a friend or relative. When I discuss this with Svandís, she explains, When you bump into someone you know in town, you simply nod your head and smile. When this happens in another city, you greet each other and ask how you are doing. When it's in another country, you hug and kiss and share a drink or a meal.

Later that day, Anna drives me to the Reykjavík Art Institute. As much as I'm interested in art, I haven't had the chance to visit many art museums before. Anna jokes about taking me to see an American artist's exhibit in Iceland. The show is very modern, bizarre, abstract art. Anna and I have a good laugh while we sit on a bench directly in front of one of the paintings and ponder the meaning. Anna is trying hard to make me feel welcome. Sharing art and laughter with her gives me a greater sense of belonging and reminds me of the fun times I've shared uncontrollable laughter with my sisters.

Anna is a most creative and kind-hearted soul. She is working hard to ensure that I am enjoying my stay and wants to help me with my classes. Her English is good, yet she is conscientious about talking to me in Icelandic. She gives me the utmost credit that if I hear it enough, eventually, I will understand it.

Once we've had enough of the abstract art, we visit Anna's friend Erla. Inside Erla's apartment, we're all laughing and having fun. Her apartment has the customary china cabinet full of Icelandic knickknacks, including vases made of volcanic lava and dishware with geographic names of Iceland printed on them. Since I do not want to drink caffeine this late at night, I turn down Erla's offer of coffee.

I'm noticing how much coffee Icelanders drink. A good cup of coffee seems to be a bonus for visiting. Erla and her husband are shocked that I could turn down such an appealing offer. I watch as they place a sugar cube between their upper and lower front teeth while sipping coffee. The hot coffee causes the sugar cube to dissolve and provides sweetness with every sip. This technique intrigues me, and I watch closely to see how it's done. When they use up the first cube before the cup is empty, they take another. I might need to start drinking coffee so I can learn to imitate this.

We are going to an outdoor swimming pool on this cold and rainy day. Birgir explains that the swimming pool is heated with geothermal water. Once we arrive at the pool building, I feel like a puppy dog walking closely behind Ásta Margrét, not knowing where to go or what to do. When we enter the shower in the women's dressing room, I notice no one is wearing a swimsuit. I fear I will have to swim in the nude. I'm relieved to discover I do wear a swimsuit, just not until taking a shower.

Outside in the pool area, my fingers feel frozen. I follow Ásta Margrét as we run and jump into the large, heated swimming pool. It feels deliciously warm on my icy, cold skin. I smile at the unusual sight of steam rising over the top of the entire swimming pool. When I swim twenty laps, the pool's warmth soothes my whole body, even in the cold rain-filled air.

Ásta Margrét informs me, The pool is open year-round.

I tell her, The outdoor swimming pools in Wisconsin are only open during the summer and close whenever it starts to rain.

We both laugh when she says, If they did that here, they'd always be closed.

On the return trip to Borgarnes with Anna and her kids, we make a routine stop at the Nesti gas station and convenience store at Hvalfjörður (Whale Fjord). Although I oppose hunting whales, I'm still eager to see the station to take slides for my dad, who teaches a university course on endangered species. When I cross the road to the station, I'm half running, with the wind pushing me the other half. The strong wind has forced Anna and the kids to return to the car. I try not to think about the blustery wind as I take photos of the vast piles of bloody whale meat.

My hair is blowing wildly, whipping across my eyes, making it challenging to compose a picture. I try hiding behind my camera lens to avoid seeing and smelling the giant slabs of red whale meat. I walk closer to the workers who are slicing away at the carcasses. The ground is slimy and slippery, and the wind pushes me along, making me feel I might blow straight into the sea. The station workers peer up at me. No one says anything. I take an entire roll of slides, then change the film and take another roll, plus a whole roll of prints. My fingers and ears are numb, but I would have taken even more photos if I had more film with me. As we drive on, I'm happy to think of the whale slides I can share with my dad.

A loud, thumping noise is coming from outside of Anna's Volvo. It's yet another flat tire, and Anna is having difficulty changing it. A truck comes by, and Anna motions for the driver to stop. Once again, I'm reminded of just what a small country Iceland is. The three men who jump out of the truck to help are from Borgarnes, so of course, Anna knows them.

The men laugh when they discover the front tire on the other side is also flat. Anna has a tube of repair glue that comes out as a white foam. The instructions are in English, and Anna expects me to explain how to use the glue. I want to be helpful, only the directions don't make sense to me. The men do something to the tire without the instructions. Whatever they've done seems to have worked. I'm relieved to return to the warm car and Borgarnes in one piece.

As it has become my daily habit, I'm writing in my journal in my bedroom when I hear Ásta talking on the phone. It's fun to be able to decipher a bit of her conversation, only not when I hear her saying something about going out. I'm hoping it doesn't involve me since I'm tired and want to go to bed. I hear Ásta call out my name. She puts on her coat and motions for me to put mine on. I have no choice but to go, wherever it might be.

We arrive at her friend Sigga's house. Ásta hands me something to taste. When I put it in my mouth and try to chew it, I discover it isn't chewable, and when I find I can't swallow it whole, I find the solution is to spit it out onto a napkin. This is the first time I've tried shark meat, and I've found a type of food in Iceland that I cannot eat.

Sigga's daughter, Ágústa, and her girlfriend, Elisabet, arrive, and Ásta pushes me out the door with them. Ágústa drives us to the movie theater. As we squeeze in through the front door, I'm shocked at how loud and smoky it is inside.

I hear a loud bass guitar coming from inside the movie theater, making me realize we're going to listen to a live band rather than watch a movie. I comb my hair in the bathroom when a girl who is already drunk offers me a tall green bottle of alcohol. I take a whiff and then a tiny sip, feeling lucky that the taste isn't too terrible. We talk in the movie theater room and sit on the edge of the stage that hosts the band. The music is so loud that I can't tell whether the lyrics are in Icelandic or another language.

A man some years older than me comes over and says something to me. The girls tell me he's asking me to dance. I agree to. I wish I hadn't when he holds me too close and forcefully kisses me. This is nothing like the first kiss I've dreamed of from watching romance movies.

He follows me, grabs my hand, and tries to kiss me again. A girl leans over and whispers to me in English, I think he's going to eat you up! I finally escape by running back to the bathroom.

I'm glad when the band stops and the lights come on, indicating it's time to leave. Elisabet is drunk and tripping over her feet. I hold her steady outside in the cold while Ágústa returns inside to find Elisabet's coat. The other cars must clear out of the parking lot first, so we have enough space to exit. Ágústa finally drops me off at Ásta and Jón's at three in the morning. I'm afraid they'll be worried since I was out so late. Instead, I find them dancing and singing songs with their friends, Sigga and Steinar, asking me to join them.

I wake up tired on Sunday morning and spend much of the day writing in my journal and finishing a long letter to my family. I'm nervous since school will begin tomorrow. How will I know where to go or what to do? Anna has told me that a girl who studied in Sweden will walk to school with me in the morning. She said that school will only last an hour tomorrow. That will cut down on the time the teacher will speak in Icelandic, and I won't understand—at least for one day.

———◇———

My first exposure to my new host country showed me that despite Icelanders' reputation for having a tough exterior, my host family warmed up to me quickly. I was excited to be in a new country, with the thrill of learning a new language, trying new foods, and attending various social events like a wedding in Reykjavík and a dance in Borgarnes.

Looking back, I realize my exchange did not offer any programs or services to assist me. Other foreign exchange students participated in orientations and organized social events. As one of two Rotary exchange students in Iceland that year (the other one lived in Akureyri, an eight-hour drive away), I had no other foreign students to collaborate with. I had no guidance counselor or support group to ask how I was getting on, offer language instruction, or guide me through. My host family became my support group, helping me to learn the language, cope with homesickness, and to introduce me to new friends, foods, and activities. To this day, I am deeply indebted to them.

What happened when I discovered I was in the hospital at the start of this chapter? I have more remembering to do before catching up to the hospital.

CHAPTER 2

A Letter Home

"Nú duga engin vettlingatök."
Literal Meaning: Now no mittens will do.
Intended meaning: When you want to do something well, take your mittens off and do it carefully and properly.

When I returned to Borgarnes from Reykjavík that Saturday evening, I was delighted to find letters from Wisconsin waiting for me. Besides the journals I kept, I wrote letters to family and friends whenever I could find the time. Although I wrote my letters in English, many Icelandic words started to creep in. Here is the letter I wrote home that last weekend before starting school, reflecting on some of the activities in Chapter 1, plus a few additional ones.

Saturday Evening, October 1, 1977

Hello Family!

Tonight, when I returned from Reykjavík, I found 2 letters on my desk from Robin and Mom written on September 17 and 18. I waited so long to write because I wasn't in Borgarnes when the letters arrived. And then Ásta told me there were four more letters down at the post office – so I ran down there to get them – and golly gee whiz! Letters from Dad, Dana, Starker, and Sayward! They were all so wonderful. I was just laughing and crying at the same time! So much news at once. And everyone is so nice, helpful, and thoughtful. While I write this, I cry to think about it.

Well, I went to the wedding, which was quite a mistake! During the whole night, I talked once to a man who spoke some English. The rest of the night, I had to keep coughing to be sure I still had a voice and to let others know I really was alive! I decided I didn't really miss anything by not understanding a word that was spoken. And I think it was foolish to go to a wedding where I didn't even know the people getting married.

I never know what is happening when I get in a car to go somewhere. I'm never quite sure just where I'm going. Then that makes things more exciting, I suppose!

On Sunday, we went to Ásta's Uncle's house. He has a son who is 17, plays the piano, and speaks some English. I had a good talk with him, and we had some delicious ice cream. The son goes to school from 2 p.m. until 7 p.m. Because too many students are in the school, they must divide the time.

Sunday night, Birgir, Ásta Margrét and I went to the Reykjavík Iðkinning Fair, an Industrial fair. This was very crowded but quite interesting. Every industry in Reykjavík was represented with a booth, including furniture, light fixtures, kitchen appliances, fur and wool clothing, rope, metal tubing, and Opal candy which tastes like cough drops, and everyone here seems to love it.

Also, I'm amazed at the number of dairy products! Yes, Iceland has many cattle and dairy farms, along with sheep. In a store, you may purchase yogurt, skýr, ymir, súr mjólk, ný mjólk, and hundreds of kinds of cheese in shrimp style, walnut, mushroom, and even green pepper.

I've had a hard time finding the differences between these varieties of yogurts and dairy products – but I've decided that if there is a difference, it's minimal. Anyway, they're all very delicious! I'm told that many of these products have just recently come out in the last five to six years. Now they have even more flavors. Also, there are all different flavors and types of ice cream.

While I'm on the topic of food, tonight at supper, I told them that my mom was afraid I was getting fat. They all thought this very funny. Ásta has been so worried. She thinks I'm eating so little! Everything tastes fine, but there are so many bready foods like toast and potatoes and very few vegetables. We have fish, pork chops, and lamb chops as the main course. For some reason, the only kind of soup Ásta buys is cream of cauliflower, even when the grocery store sells many other types.

At Svandís' apartment, I made pizza! It didn't look anything like any pizza you've ever seen, but they thought it tasted good. They had never had pizza before, so they had nothing to compare it to. I don't think they'd be very good as exchange students because they're not very willing to try new things, especially the kids. I might be introducing them to more new things than they are to me. The other day I made our famous green jello, and they liked it very much, luckily! If it wouldn't be too much trouble, could you please send the recipes to that orange drink (you know the one, Dana), shrimp quiche, chocolate chip cookies, apple pie (they've never heard of it), pizza (I didn't really know the recipe), rice crispy bars, chocolate marshmallow frosting (it's in the green recipe box). And then, if you can't send these all at once, you could send these sometime later: Mexican wedding cakes, nutmeg feather cake, pumpkin pie, banana bread, and if you think of anything else.

But it's expensive to make any of these recipes. For example, to make the green jello, the jello was 50 cents, the sour cream $1.50, canned pineapple $1.60, and I bought the small-sized containers. The marshmallows were $1.60 for the bag. I'm told that a can of corn costs $3.50 if you can believe this!

Getting back to the Industrial Fair, I took some photos using the flash which made people stare at me. We went to a fashion show, and the models performed different dances in the clothing they were modeling, featuring beautiful Icelandic wool and furs.

I guess I'm going to be talked into buying a raincoat. But the ones Svandís and Ásta Margrét showed me were just ugly! I won't consent to purchase something like that.

For breakfast, they put caviar out of a tube on their toast. I still haven't decided whether to try it. I remember one time when Mom brought some caviar home from school, and I had to wash my mouth out after trying it. All the kids here seem to love it!

Every day now, I've been going through my Icelandic lesson book. It's fun to read and work on. I find I can read and understand it much better than speaking it at this point.

Monday, we went downtown. Svandís and I took the elevator to the top of the main church. It was a fantastic sight. I could see all of Reykjavík, and the film didn't last long in the camera while my finger was busy on the little button that goes click!

Monday night, a friend of Svandís' came over. She spoke excellent English since she worked in New York City for a year. I've noticed something funny is the way all the Icelanders I've met who speak English call the sheep, "sheeps." And this friend told me she worked in a beauty "saloon."

Tuesday, we went to a Folk Museum similar to Heritage Hill State Park in Green Bay, with several old buildings restored as museums. They were closed for the winter, but I took photos of the outside. They were very handsome buildings with grass huts used to store potatoes. One building was open for the Industrial Fair, so I took photos of people making shoes and weaving using the old methods.

Tuesday night, I went with Anna to her best friend's apartment. This night was one of my best. I've never laughed so hard. The friend and her husband spoke English and have a very good sense of humor. The funniest thing was the article they shared with me called "The Awful Icelandic language." I never laughed so hard from reading something. I just love the article, and I'll send a copy to you. I don't know if it will be as funny to you as it was to me. If you could realize how well the writer put precisely how I've felt into words.

Wednesday afternoon, I went swimming with Ásta Margrét. It was freezing outside, about 30 degrees F. The pool was about 70-75 degrees F. Also, it was raining outside. I told Ásta Margrét that they close the pools in Green Bay when it rains. Ásta Margrét said to me if they did that here, the pools would always be closed! Then we went over to the three hot pools where the water is from 102-112 degrees F. This comes directly from the hot springs. Steam comes up from the water, so you can't see the other side while you swim in the pool.

Thursday and Friday morning, I went swimming again with Svandís and another friend of hers. Thursday afternoon, we went downtown to buy material for Svandís to make quilt covers for her kids. We also picked up some fabric, since Ásta is making a skirt for me. It will be like Ásta Margrét's, a beige color on which Ásta will embroider colorful flowers.

During my stay at Svandís' apartment, Linda Björg, in some extraordinary way, took my two hair combs and put them somewhere that I still haven't found and had to leave Reykjavík without them.

As you can see, I've been quite busy in Reykjavík, and many people ask me, would you rather be in Reykjavík rather than Borgarnes? Well, I can't really say. Who knows at this point?

I've been asking everyone I've met if they know anything about Icelandic folk dances, and sooner or later, I should be getting closer to finding out about them. I met a boy who was an exchange student in the United States, and his father is a ballroom dance teacher who knows some folk dances. Maybe I'll learn some yet.

Friday night, Birgir took Ásta Margrét and me out on a boat. I don't know what word to use to describe it. It wasn't huge, but not a tiny motorboat either. Birgir uses it to go out to large ships to check them for customs. I kept chewing gum since the ride was much like a roller coaster! The water was rough and would spurt up and cover the whole boat and windows. It was exciting.

Saturday, today, I left with Anna and her two kids, and we headed back to Borgarnes. I was so glad she decided not to take the Akraborg ferry home since this meant we could go past the whale station. I was so anxious to get there to get photos for you, dad. Was it ever freezing cold and windy! My fingers were so frozen I could hardly advance the film. I took pictures of the workers throwing the cut-up pieces of whales in bins and the truck picking up the bins.

After stopping at the whale station, we drove until Anna realized she had a flat tire. It was awful to have this happen again on the way back, with the weather so cold and windy. Anna couldn't figure out how to change it until a truck came along and stopped to help change the tire. Unbelievably, we discovered that the tire on the other side was also flat. Anna had a tube of repair glue that they used to mend the tire, and we made it back to Borgarnes.

Last night while I was writing this letter (it's now Sunday morning), Ásta came into my room and said something to me about "komdu út" (come out)? I asked, "núna" (now)? It was 11 p.m. and I was planning to go to sleep early since I was tired and had a headache and was anxious to write some letters. I wouldn't have believed what I was to end up doing the rest of the evening. I got into the car, I don't know why I ever did that, and we went to Sigga's where I practice the piano. I thought I would have to sit there all night, but then they pushed me out the door with their daughter and her friend, who are both 21 years old. I learned I was to go dancing with them!

This wasn't exactly what I had in mind for the night. Well, I went. I decided I had to try to have fun. It was so smoky and crowded, and everyone was pushing to get inside. I danced with them all night to crummy music with old-time songs. I tried talking with the girls. They understood very little English, and it was impossible to hear. We didn't get home until 3 a.m., and I couldn't wait to get to bed when who do you think was up dancing and singing at the house but Ásta, Jón, and their good friends Sigga and her husband. I was forced to dance and sing along with them even when I wanted to go to bed. It was okay when I knew the songs, but otherwise, not so fun. Finally, I got into my room and away from the partiers at 3:30 a.m., when I allowed myself to read all your letters once more.

I start school in Borgarnes tomorrow at 10 a.m. I hope, just hope it's good because then everything will be all right. Everyone I talk to likes Ásta and Jón so much and thinks they are wonderful and doing everything to help me. I have beautiful scenery to look out on all day long. Today, the weather is very sunny, and everyone is very friendly to me. What more could I ask for?

I've started to make note cards with Icelandic words on one side and the English translation on the other. I watch TV in English with Icelandic subtitles and this kind of helps me to learn more Icelandic, plus watching movies and listening to the radio. They speak fast, making it challenging to follow very much. Right now, I'm not trying that hard to speak Icelandic with Ásta and Jón since I don't have anything new to tell them. Now I understand a lot more, and I'm not sure if they know that or not?

Sunday night, Rich Man, Poor Man reruns were on TV. The TV in Borgarnes gets very poor reception, and I've learned that color TV is a very new thing here in Iceland, and almost no one has it.

Dad, you wanted to know what jobs they have in Borgarnes. There's a factory that makes fur coats and hats. I just learned that this is the biggest factory in Borgarnes. All the women I've met usually work part-time, like Anna, who works as a secretary. She tells me that Borgarnes does not have much travel by boat since the water flows the wrong way and it's too strong to go against the wind. Out on the small peninsula are Esso oil tanks, a Volvo mechanic repair shop, and what looks like a lumber company. Anna told me there is a dairy factory here as well. A short distance out of town is a gravel company, and there's the electric company, and they are building the bridge that I told you about. I'll try to learn more.

My "empty" book is almost full. Do you think it would be possible to send another one? I don't know how I'll last all year. I will end up filling about 50!

Sending you all my love, Paula

———◇———

This is just one of many letters home. I also recorded "letters" by taping my voice onto cassettes and exchanging those with my family. Forty-plus years later, it's hard to imagine that at the age of 16, the primary method of communication with my family in Wisconsin was by letter. In 1977, we had no email, texting, cellphones, Facetime, or Zoom, and the cost of an overseas phone call was prohibitive. It wasn't until Christmas that we first spoke by telephone.

CHAPTER 3

On Studying Fifth-Year Bookkeeping

"Ég kem alveg af fjöllu."
Literal meaning: I come completely from the mountains.
Intended meaning: I have no idea what people are talking about.

Ready or not, I start school in Borgarnes today. After living here for a month, I know much more Icelandic than when I first arrived. I've been working daily with self-created flashcards and practicing with Ásta each evening. I still have less than kindergarten-level comprehension. I can only imagine what my first day of school will bring.

Two girls knock at the front door. They are sisters. One studied in Sweden last year and knows a little English in addition to Swedish. When we reach the Borgarnes school grounds, I imitate the others as they sit on benches on the playground to await the start of school. The two sisters greet five other girls, all fourteen years old. They look dismayed when I explain that I'm sixteen. At that age, two years puts us miles apart.

When the school bell rings, I imitate the girls as they take off their shoes and stack them in a pile inside the entranceway. The students proceed to their assigned classrooms while I wonder where to go. The sisters point to a teacher who directs me to a doorway. The teacher tells me in English, You go in there. Welcome to Iceland!

Taking a deep breath, I muster up the nerve to enter the classroom and sit at an empty desk among the other twelve students. They all stare at me. I hear a few faint whispers over the stark silence. A tall, slender, red-haired teacher with a slight goatee enters and speaks to the class in Icelandic. Then he turns to me and asks me questions in English.

How long are you going to be at this school?

Until January, at least that's what I'm told.

Are you going to learn Icelandic?

I'm trying.

The teacher begins with an introduction to the class. I don't know what he's saying. I imagine he's covering the typical first-day-of-school dialogue. He hands out copies of the class schedule. A couple of the course names are similar enough to English. I'm not sure about the rest. I look them all up in my new heavy three-inch-thick Icelandic-English dictionary I've lugged with me: German, Danish, Icelandic, English, business, typing, mathematics, gym, and bookkeeping. Not a bad schedule, I think ruefully, other than I won't be able to follow any class except English.

A much older, thin man with gray fringe around his balding head enters the room. His age, stateliness, and the gold emblem on his blazer make me think he must be the principal. He introduces himself to me in English, telling me he's the "schoolmaster," using the British term. He asks each of the twelve students their names. Then he comes over to my desk and writes the title of a book for me, *Laxdæla Saga*. He explains to me that the book is available in English. I appreciate the individual attention he's giving me.

The schoolmaster leaves the classroom and is replaced by a much younger male teacher with the typical Icelandic pale skin and blond hair. This teacher seems unaware that I'm not Icelandic as he speaks for five minutes in front of the class. The only word I can make out is *heim* (home) as the twelve students stand up and file out of the classroom. I would have liked to have found out whether I need to return to school today. No one's left to ask, so I head outside toward home. On second thought, I'll go chat with Anna since she knows some English.

Two blocks later, I show Anna my schedule. She complains to me in English, You have too many language classes that you'll have no use for, like fifth-year Danish. I'd rather you had classes like Icelandic history, geography, and cooking.

Her suggestions are intriguing, only I don't know how that would be possible. The phone rings, and it's Ásta. She has ESP as to where to find me. Anna explains that Ásta will phone the schoolmaster to ask what I'm supposed to do. When I return to Ásta's and show her my schedule, she complains, just like Anna, about all the language classes I must take. I nod in agreement to whatever she's said.

As I write in my journal, I'm reminded of my cousin, Pavel, who came from Czechoslovakia with his parents to live in Manitowoc, Wisconsin, in 1969 when he was thirteen years old. At the time, I had no idea what he was going through. He quickly picked up English. He was younger than I am now. I hope I can do as well with Icelandic.

I'm so frustrated that I'd like to close my bedroom door and cry, but instead, I finish writing a sad letter home and walk with Ásta to the post office to mail it. We enter the *Kaupfelag* Department Store, run by a Rotarian. He speaks to me in English.

How's school?

I think it'll be rather tricky, I tell him, especially Danish, when the others in my class have already studied it for four years.

I think you can just choose not to take it.

Easy for him to say. I don't know how that would work.

Just as apprehensive on the second day of school, I stack my shoes in the pile at the entranceway and sit on the hallway benches upstairs with the fourteen-year-olds. The schoolmaster arrives and speaks to the class in Icelandic, The first class is canceled since the book for business class hasn't arrived yet.

I don't understand this until he translates for me. He hands me a typing book and speaks to me painfully slowly. Either he doesn't know English that well, or else he thinks he has to speak slowly in English since I don't know Icelandic.

In the hallway, I ask my classmates questions in English because the schoolmaster encouraged me to do so. What class is next? How do you like studying Danish?

The students give me blank looks and make me feel foolish when I don't get a single response. I give up and wait in silence until the Danish teacher arrives. He writes Danish vocabulary words on the board with their Icelandic translation, then turns to me and translates them into English. I move my desk closer to the girl sitting near me to share her book. The fact that I'm taking fifth-year Danish seems ironic when I barely know any Icelandic.

The Danish teacher explains to me in English that Denmark ruled Iceland from 1814 to 1918, and Iceland continued to be in union with Denmark until 1944. While the pronunciation is quite different, some Danish words resemble Icelandic. All Icelanders are required to study Danish at school. So far, I haven't met an Icelander who would admit they know any Danish. They make a sour face to indicate that they don't like it.

The time between classes at high school in Green Bay gave students a chance to go to their lockers and progress to another classroom. Here, we spend our breaks in the hallway, waiting for the next teacher to arrive.

A teacher enters the classroom for typing class. She's tall and thin, in her mid-40s, with blue eyes, Icelandic pale skin, and blonde hair. She tells me that I will need a typewriter and asks if I've ever taken typing before. I admit I haven't. Ásta told me I can use Árni's portable. The teacher goes on to speak to the class in Icelandic, and I don't understand a thing. During the break in the hallway with my classmates, I listen to them talk amongst themselves, taking in little.

Fifteen long minutes later, we re-enter the classroom for English. As soon as the dark-haired, bearded teacher enters the room, he speaks in English.

Someone in here is not Icelandic! Then he looks directly at me and asks, Why did you choose Iceland? Where are you from?

He holds up a map of the United States. I point to Green Bay and Lake Michigan and describe the weather while he translates what I say into Icelandic. He continues to talk with me in English.

You'll be a tremendous help to the class since the students are afraid to speak English. You'll help liven things up and make them eager to talk. The teacher turns to the students. Did you understand what I said?

A boy named Pálmi raises his hand to indicate he does. I guess he's the one I should try to talk to. This is the first real welcome I've had in the school, making me happier to be here.

The teacher says, You're welcome to come to me whenever you need help. Have you been homesick?

Just when I read letters from home, I tell him. I've brought slides of the United States and could show them sometime.

Ásta questions me during lunch.

How do you find the meat? She has a habit of asking me this.

Very good. I'm wondering what kind of meat it is. It's tender and flavorful.

My dear *Pála*, how do you like it?

She's making me curious, so I ask her what it is.

She whispers in my ear, It's whale meat.

This is unsettling to me since I'm concerned about the endangerment of whales. Now I feel so guilty. I've eaten whale meat and enjoyed it before I knew what it was.

Ásta says, I was afraid to tell you since I was afraid you wouldn't like it. People must learn to eat it.

I'm not sure if she realizes it's not the taste I didn't like but the thought of eating an endangered species.

When I return to school after my guilt-laden lunch, I discover an empty hallway without students. A teacher comes up the stairs and speaks to me in English, Didn't anyone tell you? Classes are canceled for the rest of the day.

Back at the house, Ásta calls Anna. I explain to Anna which textbooks I need. I tell Anna I'd rather take fifth-year Danish than nothing at all.

An Icelandic phrase I'm becoming very familiar with is *Elsku Pála mín, komdu að borða* (My dear Paula, come to eat)! Either Ásta or Jón shouts this out several times a day, calling me to the kitchen table. During dinner, I try using some new Icelandic words I've picked up while studying with Ásta. I'm pleased with my use of the new vocabulary word *fyrirgevðu,* which means "excuse me," with its strange spelling and lispy pronunciation. When Ásta thanks me for helping with the dishes, I run to my room to look up "you're welcome," which I discover is another mouthful of lispy-sounding words *ekkert að þakka.* I reassure myself that I'm learning Icelandic.

Something important in my grammar book about Icelandic pronunciation is that two letters in the alphabet, ð (eth) and þ (thorn), represent the English "th" sound. The first one is voiced, and the second one is unvoiced. With all these "th" sounds, several words and phrases come out sounding like I'm speaking with a lisp. My new favorite phrase is *Það er nefnilega það* which has four "th" sounds and translates as "that is namely that." This phrase is not especially useful. However, I love practicing all the "th" sounds.

Ásta and I review my flashcards. I try to get her to say the English words on the backside. She has difficulty pronouncing them. I try to tell her in Icelandic, Now you can understand the difficulty I'm having. Except I don't think she understood.

The schoolmaster enters the classroom with a children's book tucked under his arm. He starts dictating sentences from *Laxdæla Saga* to the other students. Then he turns to me and opens a page in the children's book, saying, Write out the words in Icelandic and then translate them into English.

He comes to check on me in between his Icelandic dictation to the rest of the class. He pages through the children's book and reads a passage aloud to me. Then he explains to the rest of the class what I'm learning. While I appreciate his attention, I laugh to myself when he uses old English words like "lass, lassie, and frock." I feel embarrassed having a young children's story read aloud to me during a high school class.

The students get out their German books as the tall, mustached teacher asks them to take turns reading German passages aloud from the book. I can translate German words that resemble English but don't know the pronunciation. The teacher writes new vocabulary words on the board. When the class is over, he tells me, You must know all the new vocabulary words by tomorrow.

I'm ready to leave for gym class after lunch. Ásta tells me to wait. She pages through the photo album I brought from Wisconsin and points to a photo of me in my ballet bodysuit. She says, You need a bodysuit like this for gym.

Ásta calls a shop to let them know I'll be stopping in. I'm nervous now since I'll be late for class. The clerk at the shop holds up a black bodysuit to check the size. She spends a long time folding and packaging it. I scoop up the bag and speed out the door as the school bell rings.

Racing up the school stairs, I see the schoolmaster and call out to him in English, Where do I go for gym class?

I follow him to a building hidden behind the side of the school. Once inside, the girls take off their shoes, so I do the same. I notice they leave their regular street clothes on. It seems the bodysuit I rushed to purchase isn't needed today.

Sitting on the side with the girls, the teacher calls off numbers. I am *seytyan* (seventeen). The teacher gives instructions that aren't clear to me. All the girls take off their socks, so I do. They get into position and begin catching and throwing a ball, trying to hit each other with it. *Jesús og María* (Jesus and Mary) I whisper under my breath. This is the only swearing I've learned in Icelandic so far.

The game reminds me of something like dodgeball. I can't figure out the rules with my limited Icelandic. One girl throws the ball as all the other girls chase after it, first to one side, then the other. Now it's my turn to throw the ball. The player who catches the ball throws it, hitting me on my back as a student directs me to the opposite end of the gym.

At first, I think the game is over. Then I learn we're just stopping to select teams. Two students pick teams. I'm the only one left. By default, I'm sent to team two. We start throwing the ball and running. I do my best to do what I think is expected of me.

The girls put their shoes and socks back on when the game ends, so I do the same. I try to explain to the girls in Icelandic that I've never played this game before and don't know the rules. They may not have understood me, but I feel better having justified my seeming inadequacy.

I rush out the door as fast as possible in the morning to arrive in time for Icelandic class. Frustration sets in when I don't understand a word. I sit at my desk, and my mind wanders, still half asleep. Now I'm relieved to be in English class, the one subject in which I can excel. When class is over, the teacher asks me, How are you doing? He's concerned that I seem downhearted. I save face by insisting, Everything's fine. I run to catch up with Juliana, a dark-haired girl from class.

She walks toward her bright orange Volkswagen van and says to me in English, You'll come with me, so you're not alone? Feeling like she's my savior, I climb into her van and try to make conversation using the little Icelandic I know.

Juliana parks her van and leads me into a small bakery tucked upstairs off the main street. I'm delighted to share a freshly baked chocolate éclair with her, still warm from the oven.

When we return to fifth-year bookkeeping, the teacher looks at me and asks in English, Have you ever had this class?

No, I haven't, and I don't understand much.

The teacher gives us a homework assignment. I copy the questions from the book, unable to decipher a word of the long, complicated bookkeeping terms I write down.

Ásta serves lamb chops, mashed potatoes, and cauliflower, while I wonder if everyone in Borgarnes eats this much for lunch. I gather my school materials, including Árni's ten-kilo "portable" typewriter, and return to school.

My first class in the afternoon is math. What a relief since I can at least understand the numbers, even when we're working on story problems. I'm wary of typing class because the teacher was so abrupt the last time. Luckily, today, she's more approachable. She offers to give me a private lesson. She warns that she won't translate the whole book for me. I laugh, not expecting her to do that. Then I have fun typing the Icelandic exercise, regardless of whether I know the meaning of what I'm typing. The teacher tells me, You're doing well. You just need practice.

The next day, I suffer through a morning of frustration in Icelandic class and then type Icelandic characters that I'll never use. No teacher shows up for the third class. Íris and Inga, two girls in my class, find out that the teacher isn't coming and we're free to go.

We walk the two blocks to the *Kaupfelag* department store to look over paper and notebooks. Then we head downstairs to the grocery section to buy chocolate milk and Prince Polo bars. At the check-out counter, Íris is helpful when she hands me a straw, explains how much it costs, and puts the chocolate milk in a bag. We return to school and sit upstairs in the hallway, sipping the milk and munching on our chocolate. I try to converse with the girls about school activities, dances, and travels using the few Icelandic phrases I've learned so far. I'm happy to hear their cheerful responses.

On my walk home, Anna drives by and stops to give me a ride. She talks to me in Icelandic.

You're going to Reykjavík today to a wedding?

No, I don't know anything about a wedding.

You won't be going to school this afternoon. Ásta called to tell them you wouldn't be there.

I discover Anna is teasing me about going to another wedding since she knows how painful the last one was for me. She reassures me, You'll go to Reykjavík, but you don't have to go to the wedding.

As soon as we arrive at Birgir and Svandís' apartment, I learn that they've arranged for me to go to a school dance with Ásta Margrét. When I see that Ásta Margrét's been crying, I worry she doesn't want me to go with her. If Svandís made her invite me, I'd rather not go. Svandís says, You shouldn't feel bad about Ásta Margrét's moodiness. It's something between Ásta Margrét and me.

I feel left out. It might be too personal to share with me. Two of Ásta Margrét's friends come to the door, and we leave for the school dance. When we arrive, a DJ is playing records on the stage, with students already dancing. Ásta Margrét introduces me to two more of her friends, one who lived in Canada for two years. When I see Ásta Margrét putting on her coat, I'm elated since I think we're leaving and I put my coat on too. Then she continues dancing. I have no choice but to keep dancing in my coat. After hours of heated agony, we head home.

As we enter the apartment, Ásta asks me, *Gaman elskan* (fun dear)? It's easiest to agree, so I nod and head to the TV room to sleep on the sofa. Ásta and Svandís shout from the kitchen, *Heyrðu elskan* (Hey dear), come talk with us. Since I'm tired from the uncomfortable evening at the dance, I'm in no mood to converse. I tell them firmly, *Goða nott* (Good night)!

Svandís, the kids, and I snack on brownies and milk in the kitchen while Ásta and Jón prepare for the wedding I'm not obliged to attend. Ásta and Jón come out of the guest room looking smart in their wedding outfits. The bright blue sky looks even more inviting since I don't have to go to the wedding.

In my free time, I practice Icelandic phrases from the grammar book while watching an Icelandic TV show. Svandís serves us all ice cream. During the TV commercials, I talk with Svandís about Christmas in Iceland.

Svandís says, Here we celebrate Christmas for three days. I'm not sure why. Maybe because there's nothing else to do.

I explain to Svandís that my whole family is always together every Christmas. Then I feel a twinge of homesickness, thinking how that won't happen this year. I console myself that it shouldn't hurt too much since we'll have so many fun activities here.

I wake up in the morning at nine, ready to go for a walk. I wait until Svandís is up to tell her I'm heading out. As soon as I step outside, I smell the chilly air and feel the crisp, cool Icelandic freshness I'm becoming familiar with. The clear day gives me a wonderful sense of freedom from any inside responsibilities, like the pressure of school and learning Icelandic.

Without warning, my feet switch from a brisk walk into an invigorating run, and I speed far out onto the narrow pier about a mile from Birgir and Svandís' apartment toward the lighthouse. I brush my feet close to the seaweed on the sandy pier and smell the fresh sea breeze, thinking how lucky I am to be here.

Exhilarated by my walk, Svandís asks me if I'd like to go with her to the bakery. Ásta Margrét and Linda Björg come along as well. The sweet-smelling pastries remind me of my mom's home-baked Czech *kolače* and makes me long for home. Svandís drives us to a park in downtown Reykjavík to eat our fluffy white meringue. Afterward, we walk to the fountain, and I admire the view of the ducks and swans swimming in the city park. The swans frame a delicate reflection in the pond in front of the parliament building.

In contrast to the frustration and struggles with school and the language, the warmth of the bright sun on my face makes me happy to be living here in Iceland. Breaking through the ice to get to know people is challenging. However, I'm starting to feel a strong connection with my host family and the mountainous lava landscapes that decorate this unique island.

Ásta and I are chatting in front of the evening TV news at Svandís and Birgir's apartment. Ásta says, Do you want to go to the movie?

Not really, I want to watch *Rich Man, Poor Man* (a rerun, at least for me) on TV.

You'll be going with my nephew, Gylfi.

I immediately change my mind and tell her I'll go. I dress in my red turtleneck under my black, grey, and red print pullover sweater, nervous about going to Gylfi's house. I try to talk with Gylfi in the living room with his mother, grandfather, and other visitors. Gylfi puts on the customary dark navy-blue wool coat that the young guys wear here—which I have a weakness for as he looks exceptionally handsome in it.

On the drive to the theater, I enjoy Gylfi's mild flirting and the amusement of flirting back. He stops to pick up two of his male friends, and the four of us enter the movie theater together. I learn that we're seeing the movie *The Groove Tube*, a 1974 American comedy starring Chevy Chase. The poster outside advertising the film describes it as "Amazingly funny."

It turns out the movie isn't as funny as the review advertised. When it's over, I sit in the backseat of the car with two of Gylfi's friends, while another, who also doesn't speak English, sits in the front. Gylfi drives around the city as we listen to old songs sung in English on the radio like *You Are My Sunshine.*

When I sing along, Gylfi asks, Are these American songs since you know them? I prefer jazz.

Gylfi stops at a store so one of his friends can buy *pylsur* (hot dogs). The friend shouts to me in Icelandic.

What do you want on it, everything?

Sure, I say. Proud to understand the question.

Gylfi makes another stop to buy Cokes. He speaks to me in English again.

Do people drive around at home at night, go to parties, or drink beer and smoke grass? Have you tried grass?

No, I reply. And you?

No, I probably would if I had the chance. Beer is outlawed in Iceland, so unless the beer is homemade, it's more common to drink hard liquor.

When Gylfi drops me off at Svandís and Birgir's apartment, he gives me his hand to shake as I get out of the car. I tell him in Icelandic, I had a fun time. Maybe I'll see you again sometime.

I run up the stairs to find Svandís, Birgir, Ásta, and Jón in the kitchen talking. And then, the same question, *Gaman elskan* (fun dear)?

Birgir teases me in English, You have yourself some boyfriends?

I just laugh and say, *Goða nott.* Then I think about Gylfi as I'm trying to get to sleep.

Svandís picks me up from my orthodontist appointment to adjust my braces. We stop at the grocery store, where she sees a woman she knows. I'm pleased to follow a good deal of their conversation as they discuss the possibility of an upcoming nationwide strike.

Svandís explains the strike to me, They don't know how long it'll last. It's proposed to begin at midnight tonight. There won't be any mail, bus, or telephone service, and no school on Thursday, including all of Iceland! We couldn't manage if everything closed for too long, but I don't think it will. If there's a strike, I'll come to Borgarnes with the kids.

She offers to prepare an Icelandic specialty of boiled sheep's head with oatmeal and sheep's blood. She asks, Do you know what we do with that?

Drink it? I ask.

Nei, nei (no, no). She laughs. We use it to make blood pudding.

When we return to Borgarnes, I ask Ásta to call the schoolmaster to find out when school will start tomorrow. But the radio informs us that the countrywide strike has officially begun. Schools and businesses will most likely be closed for at least a week. Ásta, Jón, and I watch the news on TV. The Icelandic President Kristján Eldjárn explains that there will be a strike, with no school, no TV, and no radio. I add, *Ekkert að gera* (nothing to do).

Svandís and the kids have arrived to wait out the strike. I appreciate Ásta Margrét's invitation to go on a walk with her and her two girlfriends. I can see why it might not be her first choice to invite me along, this American exchange student who is two years older than her and barely knows Icelandic. Not only is it difficult to grasp what they're talking about, but also to comprehend how they can enjoy walking the entire ring of Borgarnes in this freezing weather. Once we return to the house, my body is cold all the way through to my bones. I study from my Icelandic language book for the rest of the day. After dinner, I put on my flannel pajamas and head straight to bed.

I have no idea what's in store for today until Ásta invites me to the Borgarnes' slaughterhouse. We'll purchase sheep innards to make the Icelandic specialty Svandís has raved about called *slátur* (slaughter). Svandís smacks her lips as she explains to me that she will also make *blóðmör* (blood pudding) and *lifrapylsa* (liver sausage). I can tell these are some of her favorite foods from the expression on her face and the way she flutters her eyelashes. I'm intrigued at the prospect of sampling yet some more new foods.

At the slaughterhouse, Jón introduces me to his cousin, who hands me a long white butcher jacket to wear during the tour. Jón's cousin explains the slaughtering process to me in simple English, We start with the sheep. Then they use a gun and shoot them. It's all done quickly.

I see the workers ripping the skins, cutting the head off, then the limbs.

Jón's cousin explains, The meat is sent downstairs and cut up even more.

The sight of the bloody sheep's limbs is gruesome, and the stench makes breathing difficult. I focus on taking photos instead of the blood and the stench.

Jón's cousin continues, The only part of the sheep thrown out is the wool from the sheep's head. The waste is used as feed for animals.

As we proceed into the adjoining room, I must walk straight across the bloody floor. With this putrid smell penetrating my nostrils, I don't think I'll be able to eat for a week.

A female worker points to me and tells Svandís in Icelandic, She's one American in a thousand who will ever see this.

Lucky me.

As difficult as it was to see and smell the bloody sheep, our slaughterhouse tour is followed by sweets at home during *kaffi* (coffee). Then I go with Svandís, Ásta Margrét, and Linda Björg to the local wool shop. The tiny room is crowded with tightly packed sewing machines, as women are busily sewing woolen coats, hats, and scarves. They smile at my interest. I'm astounded by the mounds of woolen goods piled up alongside each machine, ready to be sewn.

I'm concerned about picking anything out in case I haven't brought enough money. It turns out I'm in luck since the wool pieces I've selected are only 500 Icelandic *krónur* (about $12) each. Ásta examines the wool I purchased to see how she will use it to make hats and scarves to send home to my family.

Since my host parents know I play the piano, my Danish teacher, Jón Björnsson (whose first and last name is identical to my host father's), telephones to ask if I would like to come for a piano lesson. When I meet him at the school building, he directs me to a house across from the school to introduce me to the piano teacher.

In the tiny, overheated room, the piano teacher asks me formally in English, How do you do?

The Danish teacher leaves me alone with the unshaven, pot-bellied piano teacher, who tells me gruffly, Play a sonatina for me.

Another man knocks on the door. The piano teacher steps out of the house to talk with him while I play the sonatina alone. When the piano teacher returns, he lectures me in English. You must watch your hands, hold them steady and work on your rhythm since it's uneven.

He picks out a Bach Invention for me to sightread. He tells me to practice it and that we will meet for a lesson two times a week. He doesn't explain which days these will be or at what time.

At Sigga's house, I practice the Bach Invention, Monti's Czardas, and Beethoven's Moonlight Sonata on her piano. Sigga invites me to have *kaffi* with her and her daughters. Sitting together in the kitchen, I think about how the concept of "coffee" here, differs from home. Icelanders set aside time in the afternoon and call it "*kaffi*," which means coffee, regardless of whether you drink coffee, tea, milk, or something else. It feels like a whole meal rather than just a snack. We're served fruit salad. It's interesting to watch Sigga spoon the fruit on top of her bread.

The strike has dragged on for three weeks. It's already October, and I've only had one week of school so far. Svandís is leaving at *half one,* as you say in Icelandic, or twelve-thirty. It's difficult to say it this way since *half-one* sounds like it should be one-thirty. The kids are running around saying their goodbyes, *bless, bless.* I'm about to give Ásta Margrét an Icelandic kiss goodbye when she tells me she's not leaving after all. I'm always the last to know.

When I see the piano teacher outside as I near his house, he tells me he'll be there in a minute. I enter the room and start playing the Bach Invention he's assigned me. This lesson is less appealing than the last because of an even more pungent perspiration odor. Though I'm pleased with how hard I worked on this piece and how well I played it, he focuses on my few mistakes.

In the movie theater lobby that afternoon, with Ásta Margrét and her friend Helena, we buy tickets and small boxes of the well-liked Icelandic Opal licorice candy as we wait for the theater doors to open. A girl in line asks me in English, How long have you had your braces? The question comes out of nowhere. It's nice she has acknowledged my existence. As we look for our seats, I discover we're going to see an American Film, *Lady Lace.* I'm distracted during the entire movie since the guy from my class, Pálmi, is sitting nearby. He looks handsome in his navy-blue wool peacoat.

Gaman, elskan (fun, dear)? They all ask me in unison as we enter through the kitchen door, with an overpowering odor coming from the kitchen. Ásta has made an Icelandic specialty, *svið* (boiled sheep's head), for dinner. This traditional Icelandic dish involves cutting the sheep's head in half, removing the brain, and then boiling it in water. I have now discovered another Icelandic food that is unappealing to me.

I'm not partial to the waxy, chewy texture, not to mention the putrid smell. I can't figure out how to eat around the big bone on my plate. The big hole where the eye would normally be, together with the nauseating smell, doesn't make for an appetizing dinner. The rest of the family considers it a great treat. Since this is an Icelandic delicacy, I'm determined to eat it and at least give an appearance of enjoyment.

During dinner, Ásta tells me the plans have changed, and Ásta Margrét and I won't be going to a dance. What a relief. Ásta is more chatty than usual tonight and continues talking. I just say, "*já, já, já,*" while inhaling, in the typical Icelandic style known as *innsog*. This quirk of speech is a useful way to emphasize agreement and encourage whomever you're speaking with to continue talking. As Ásta and I talk about travel, I notice that whenever Icelanders refer to somewhere outside of the country, such as the United States or anywhere else, they call it "*úti*" (out).

After three weeks, the countrywide strike is over, and school will begin again. Ásta comes into my room with a pack of cigarettes, explaining that she hasn't been able to buy them with the strike on. When I say, Good, she makes a face. Then she gives me a smoke-filled Icelandic kiss on the lips.

Returning to school, the wind is fierce until I go inside and up the stairs to discover I'm the first from my class to arrive. Five minutes later, three boys and the English teacher show up. Eventually, three more girls come, leaving six who never show up. During English class, the teacher has the students read aloud from the book. When it's my turn, the teacher asks me some questions in English.

What did you do in your English class last year?

I struggle to remember, feeling good that I have at least one class I understand and can be helpful. When I respond in English, the teacher asks the students, Did you understand what she said? Again, Pálmi raises his hand. When class is over, the English teacher stops me to ask, Are you able to understand any more Icelandic?

I'm working on it.

Today when I arrive at gym class, all the girls are already wearing their black bodysuits. Once I've dressed in mine, I enter the gym and get in line with the girls. Then I follow as we march around the gym, with the teacher calling out, *Einn, tveir, einn, tveir* (One, two, one, two), like marching soldiers. I mimic the others as we run in a line, kicking our legs in front of us, making me feel a bit ridiculous. I follow along as we must walk on our toes and then run with our hands up in the air.

The gym teacher divides us into groups to do more exercises. These are more like dance steps, which I enjoy, only I'm uncomfortable in the skimpy black bodysuit. We're divided into two teams to play basketball. Ironic as it may be, coming from the United States, I've never played basketball before. I'm not familiar with the rules or how to dribble. I keep running with the ball in my hand, causing the teacher to blow her whistle at me. When we take turns shooting baskets, I'm shocked when I actually make one. Finally, we're dismissed to take showers. When the girls undress, I realize no one else is wearing a bra or underwear under their bodysuits. How was I to know?

During bookkeeping class, I can't follow what the teacher is saying, which makes me so frustrated that I'd like to throw my textbook over the fjord. I feel silly when the teacher comes over to check my work and I have none to show. What does he expect when no one helps me, and I barely know Icelandic? It seems useless to try to learn fifth-year bookkeeping in Icelandic. My hope is that I'm learning much more than bookkeeping.

Now for the climax of my Icelandic language learning so far. This morning, for the first time, after having lived here for eight weeks, I understood every word of Ásta's nonstop monologue during breakfast. What a relief to finally break out of beginner's Icelandic. Although I still write in my journal and write my letters home in English, all my conversations are now in Icelandic, and I've even begun to think and dream in Icelandic.

———◇———

As I write this memoir, both Ásta and Jón and their daughter Svandís have since passed away. It makes me sad to think about those from my host family who are no longer with us. I don't think I could have survived the school year without the support of my host family. Not only did Ásta and Jón become like my adopted parents. Svandís was like an adopted aunt, sister, and dear friend all in one. She nursed me when I was ill and pumped me up when I was down.

Starting school in Borgarnes in a new language when the students already had years of coursework behind them presented steep challenges. I couldn't read the fifth-year level textbooks, and the teachers couldn't give me a tailored curriculum. The school wasn't set up to accommodate a student who did not know Icelandic. I would have had to go into classrooms with much younger students to have a more appropriate schedule.

Learning Icelandic was an upward battle without any formal instruction. The Borgarnes schoolmaster's assistance with Icelandic grammar was minimal and short-lived. To communicate, socialize, and participate in activities, I knew I had to master the language. Despite the three-week countrywide strike with no mail and no school, I proved that I could cope with new challenges in a new culture and language. I even improved my Icelandic through frequent conversations with my host family.

CHAPTER 4

Skating on Thin Ice

"Sjaldan er ein báran stök."
Literal meaning: There is seldom a singular ocean wave.
Intended meaning: Good or back luck is often followed by the same thing, or, when it rains, it pours.

Between bookkeeping and English class, I walk down the hill with Íris and Hrönn to the *Kaupfélag* Department Store. We purchase our usual chocolate milk and Prince Polo bars. I'm becoming very familiar with these chocolate wafers, which are imported from Poland and are popular here in Iceland. Returning to school, the English teacher asks me to read a question aloud from the book. When I give my answer in English, my classmate Pálmi, teases me, *Erfitt* (difficult)? I smile and wish I knew Icelandic better so I could flirt back.

In the kitchen, over lunch, Ásta showers me with questions. How do you like the kids at school? Do you have any girlfriends? Without giving me a chance to answer, she asks, How about Íris? How do you like her? Although I sometimes walk to the store with Íris and Hrönn, with the language, age, and cultural gaps, I can't say we've reached friendship status. I'm sure these are natural questions for Ásta to ask. I can't explain how difficult it is to make friends and how lonely it is at school.

Up early on an icy cold Sunday morning, I dress in my ribbed long winter underwear beneath my jeans. Breakfast is cornflakes, although folks here call all cereal *cornflakes*, using the English word, regardless of the brand or type of cereal. At the breakfast table, Ásta tells me that she and Jón didn't get home until three in the morning since they ended up at Sigga and Steinar's house. I'm relieved I didn't go with them. While I don't have any friends my age here in Borgarnes, it isn't much fun hanging out with Ásta and Jón's older friends when I can't participate in the conversations, and they drink a lot.

Birna, the girl who lives next door, calls to ask me if I'll come skating with her and her friend and two younger sisters that afternoon. I agree to go, although I don't know what the ice skating will involve or how far away it is. Ásta calls Anna, who will loan me a pair of skates.

I dress for the excursion by adding a pair of wool socks, a wool hat, and a scarf to my usual outdoor attire. Birna's mother drives us twenty kilometers outside Borgarnes to a large, frozen lake. Instead of a man-made ice-skating rink with dozens of kids ice skating, this is a pristine setting with snow-capped mountains in the background and no sign of human life except for us and the occasional car on the road. Birna's mother waits in the car while we head over to skate on the clear lake.

My hands are already frozen as I squeeze my feet into Anna's skates which are at least a full size too small. I'm hardly a pro, but I have skated every winter since I was five. Unfortunately, the ill-fitting skates cause me to slip and struggle like I've never skated before. Birna, her two younger sisters, and her friend Helena skate faster and farther ahead of me. My hair whips around my face from the rough wind and gathers in a clump under my Icelandic wool hat. I wish I could stay in the car with Birna's mom. Ah, yes, Iceland is beautiful, only it isn't easy!

We each break off a long, clear icicle dangling near the lake's edge. It's magical to munch on the sparkly wands of ice to quench our thirst. The girls are playful as they use their scarves to take turns pulling each other. They skate over to the side and take off their skates. Hooray, we're finished! Except after switching into our shoes, we leave our skates behind, ensuring that we will return.

I'm relieved to be out of the painful skates and inside the warmth of the car. Birna's mom serves us hot chicken noodle soup from a thermos. It tastes delicious. Sadly, it's not long before I'm forced to return to the frozen lake. Squeezing my already aching feet back inside the killer skates is agonizing.

The pain increases when I realize the girls are going to skate around the lake again. I'm amazed at their willpower as they speed along in utter enjoyment. I'm far behind, unable to explain how my feet are aching since I don't have the Icelandic words.

The two older girls skate far ahead as I wobble to keep up with the younger ones. My right heel is throbbing so much that I must take baby steps. I manage to work my way over to the edge of the frozen lake to sit down. Upon returning to the car, Birna's mom offers us hot chocolate and chocolate bars, which lessens the throbbing.

As I'm dropped off, I thank them and say *mikið gaman* (very fun) as I hide my suffering. Inside the kitchen, I see a pink-frosted cake on the table, along with two letters from home. This also helps ease the pain.

When I finally get the courage to pull off my socks, my right heel is raw and bloody. Following a sleepless night, I limp into the kitchen to eat a bowl of cornflakes alone since Ásta and Jón aren't awake yet. Then I listen to silly jokes on the English Keflavík radio station: Why did the orange cry? Because the banana split. When I leave for school, the pitch-black sky makes it difficult to find my way.

The long, dark winter days have set in, resulting in much fewer daylight hours. The dreary darkness and my punctured wound make walking difficult. I manage to get through gym class, awkwardly imitating the other girls as I try to keep the weight off my right foot. When we all parade into the showers, it's unusual to see the girls' lack of inhibition or embarrassment. The girls here are more affectionate with one another than in Wisconsin. I remember how yesterday, when ice-skating, the girls held hands and hugged each other. Seeing that the girls are not shy around each other, I'm wondering how to crack through their reserve towards me.

Soon it's the weekend again. The idea of heading to Hvanneyri on this chilly morning makes me reluctant to get up. I snuggle under my blankets in bed until nine-thirty. As I help Ásta with the dishes, we discuss what I should wear to the school dance at Hvanneyri, a 30-minute drive from Borgarnes. Ásta suggests that I wear my black gaucho pants. Instead, I pack both my jeans and my baby blue rug skirt (a skirt resembling rug fabric) and then will see what the others are wearing.

While I'm the only student from Borgarnes to be invited to the dance at Hvanneyri, I'm told that girls from the nearby Varmaland sewing school will also attend. My invitation came from Magnús Magnússon, the Hvanneyri schoolmaster who is also the President of the Borgarnes Rotary Club. Whenever Jón mentions the school, he clicks his tongue like the clip-clopping of a horse to remind me that the Hvanneryri School specializes in farming.

I practice my typing until Bubbi arrives to give me a ride. The sun shines brightly as we see small white farmhouses with furry white sheep and soft brown and beige thick-haired Icelandic horses. Always willing to accommodate, he stops so I can take some close-up pictures. Bubbi's thick dark brown hair blows freely around his face, covering his dark eyes. He is quiet and reserved like his dad. I'm lucky that Bubbi and Anna have welcomed me to their house numerous times, shared meals, and entrusted their kids in my care.

We arrive at the main entrance, which looks like a newer school with its modern construction. Bubbi asks inside for the schoolmaster, unloads my luggage, and we say our goodbyes. The schoolmaster shows me to room eleven, my lodging for the night. He explains the evening plans, The students will play card games followed by a dance with the girls from the nearby Varmaland School.

Magnús asks me, Do you know how the idea for your Rotary student exchange in Borgarnes began?

I do not, but I'm eager to hear the story.

Magnús continues, My son learned about the program a year ago, applied, and was accepted. He decided against going since he didn't want to interrupt his sports program here in Iceland. As a Borgarnes Rotary member, Jón told his son Árni about the opening, and Árni ended up going instead. That left Árni's bedroom vacant for you. If it weren't for my son, you wouldn't be here in Iceland now!

I'm directed to the cafeteria for *kaffi* where I have a cup of tea with chocolate cake. I'm introduced to a male student assigned to help me with the card games since I don't know the rules. Then I follow the girls into a classroom to join in the chorus practice for an hour. Since I don't understand the lyrics, the singing gives me a chance to think about how I miss home. I wonder what my family is doing while I'm here on a gloomy day at this boarding school in the middle of nowhere.

A female student asks me the inevitable question, *Gaman* (fun)?

I say, Yes, of course. What else can I do but agree?

She then asks me to dance. We march around to a folksy Scandinavian dance, weaving in and out as couples, then raising our arms to form arches for each pair to pass under. The dance style reminds me of the Virginia Reel that we dance back home, except the tune is Scandinavian.

One of the male students invites the girl sitting next to me to dance. When she declines, I ask myself, would I say yes if he asks me, knowing he asked her first? It turns out that I would, as he does ask me to dance, and I agree. I enjoy doing a fun marching dance. I feel the palms of our hands sweating together and am nervous about the part in the dance when I must climb up onto his back. I'm pleased when I manage. The music switches to a slow dance. I'm uncomfortable dancing so close to my partner, a total stranger. I don't even know his name. When the dance is over, he says, *Takk* (thanks), and that's all the talking and dancing we do.

I lie awake in bed with thoughts buzzing through my head about the difficulties of coping in another country. It's challenging to manage in another language in an isolated boarding school with students older than me. I fall asleep until I hear a rustling noise outside my room. When I hear my door opening, I think someone is coming to wake me. I'm alarmed when I see a male student standing over my bed.

He whispers to me in Icelandic, The schoolmaster is after me since I've been drinking. If I'm discovered, I'll be sent home for two weeks.

Having been awakened by this intruder, my heart is pounding fast. I'm unsure what to do. I hear footsteps out in the hall. The stranger seems honest and sincere enough. Should I be fearful that he might try to molest me? He sits so close to me that I can smell his breath, which is thick with alcohol.

Oh, you are the American student, he whispers.

Now that he realizes I'm American, the intruder switches to broken, drunken English. I feel sorry for him when he speaks again, I hate this school. The schoolmaster has so much control. You must be in good with him to survive, and I'm not. All the students think about is work and not enough about the soul.

I don't have any experience with drunkenness except for what I've gained so far here in Iceland. The drunk student touches my hand and speaks to me in English, You're a good girl.

He holds onto both of my shaking hands to soothe me. We sit together quietly as I pull my hands away and nervously clutch the blanket on the bed to cover myself. When the sounds in the hall go away, the intruder leaves. Now it's impossible to get back to sleep.

I'm trying to decide whether to tell anyone about this episode. I don't want him to get into trouble, so I decide not to.

On Sunday morning, I walk to the nearby church with three girls I met at the dance. The church is a tiny building serving the community of Hvanneyri. The priest wears an elaborate purple robe with gold piping. Several students sing in the chorus, accompanied by an organ player. One of the girls hands me a songbook, so I try to sing along. I'm relieved when I'm able to pronounce the new, unfamiliar lyrics, perhaps because the songs are so slow. The priest doesn't have a singing voice. That doesn't stop him from belting out louder than anyone else. I learn from one of the girls that this is a Lutheran church, and ninety percent of Icelanders are Lutheran.

As the schoolmaster drives me back to Borgarnes, I think how my stay at Hvanneyri has highlighted the difficulty in talking with the students in Icelandic and trying to fit in. I feel bad for the drunk student who was eventually caught and sent home for two weeks, even with his escape to my room. Maybe he's lucky to leave for two weeks since he was so unhappy, just as I found it challenging to fit in.

Inside the warmth of Ásta's kitchen, she makes me eat again. We have dark rye bread topped with shrimp and sardines plus tomato and cucumber slices. I tell her about my adventures at Hvanneyri, leaving out the parts about trying to crack through icy student exteriors and the drunk student who entered my room in the middle of the night.

Pálmi is an excellent example of how I'm starting to break through and make friends in my Borgarnes class. He asks my classmates what score they got on their math test. Then he turns to me and says, You only missed one problem. You got the best grade in the class.

Sometimes Pálmi knows just what to say to make me feel good. Hearing that I did well on the math test is especially exciting since it consisted of complex story problems. I needed to use my thick Icelandic-English dictionary to translate all the text on the test.

He goes on to ask, What is the word *heimabakað* in English?

I tell him, *homemade.*

Pálmi says, I've been learning English for five years and didn't know that, and you know Icelandic after only two months here.

I think how good he is at giving compliments.

My classmates are talking excitedly about today's basketball tournament. I feel a knot in my stomach, worrying about when the tournament will start and what to do. When class is over, I ask Hrönn and Íris. They tell me the games will begin at one this afternoon. The knot twists tighter as I try to convince myself it will be fun.

Just before lunch, Jón brings four letters to my room from friends and family in Wisconsin. Jón says, When people write to you here, all they need to write on the envelope is Paula White, Borgarnes, Iceland, and it will get to you. That's because everyone in Borgarnes knows who you are. Even the folks at the national post office headquarters know your name.

I find a twenty-dollar bill tucked inside the letter from my parents. They sound so happy, which relieves my stress and lessens my stomachache. Lunch is another heavy meal of liver, potatoes, green peas, and cream of cauliflower soup. Then I leave for the basketball tournament.

Without enough seats for spectators, I watch the match from the narrow edge of the court. With barely enough room to stand on the sideline, students keep stepping on my feet as they pass by. I can't believe how rough these young teenage basketball players play the game. I stand watching several games in a row, glued to the same spot.

Another hour into this ordeal, the bright orange basketball comes flying directly toward me at high speed. It's coming too fast, making it impossible for me to move out of the way. Even if I had time to move, I'm crowded in by the other spectators. The basketball slams onto the right side of my head with a loud, vibrating *bam*! My entire body goes numb, and I see sparks of stars above my head, just like in a comic strip.

Two classmates run over to inquire, *Er allt í lagi* (Are you all right)? I'm so stunned that I simply nod. Bells are ringing in my ears. Everything is blurry. The darkness inside my head makes me worry about how I'll find my shoes and walk home. Stars spin around my head for another hour before I blindly hobble over to find my socks and shoes amidst all the others. Taking the stairway away from the gym, I enjoy the cool, fresh air outside.

I walk home in a daze, feeling nauseated, while Ásta insists that I sit down with her and Sigga for *kaffi*. I try to explain that I was hit in the head by the basketball and that I'm dizzy. I can't get my point across. I eat one biscuit and drink a small amount of milk without being able to focus on Ásta and Sigga's faces. Their Icelandic is even more complicated than usual. Ásta talks about going to Reykjavík. I don't respond. I leave for my room wondering, where is Reykjavík?

I lie down briefly on my bed, still feeling nauseous. Before I reach the bathroom, I throw up on the bedroom carpet and then again in the bathroom. I try rehearsing how to explain in Icelandic that I don't feel well. For a distraction, I turn the radio on. The announcer's words don't make any sense. I keep repeating what I'll say to Ásta and Jón, *Ég er svo þreytt og ég veit ekki hvað er að mér* (I'm so tired and don't know what's wrong with me). I picture Jón walking past my bedroom door. That's the last thing I can remember before waking up in a dark room from the cold wetness on my forehead.

I drift in and out of sleep, still not comprehending why I'm here. I'm thankful to discover that Ásta and Jón are real when they enter my hospital room. Ásta has brought a box of chocolates and my purple pillow cross-stitch project. She points to a cabinet where my bathrobe and toothbrush are stored. I can't believe I've spent all night and most of today in a hospital bed.

Ásta keeps asking, Do you feel dizzy? She tells me she brings greetings from the whole family. A nurse tells Ásta and Jón that I can go home since the x-rays didn't show any problems. I resent being spoken about in the third person, but I'm relieved to get the good news about going home. Earlier, I overheard a nurse saying I'd have to stay several days.

I'm quiet as Jón drives us home. I still wonder what I've just been through. I must have been in the hospital in Akranes since it didn't take as long to drive to Borgarnes as it would have from Reykjavík. The doctor's orders are that I cannot go to school tomorrow. Then Svandís calls to ask about me, and she says no one has school tomorrow since it's a holiday.

Ásta peppers me with questions. Who was with you when the basketball hit you? Did you walk home alone? Did they think it was serious right when you were hit? It didn't come all at once, did it?

I try to answer her questions. I ask myself, *what* didn't come? Since I have no idea what exactly happened to me, I try to console myself by thinking how much more exciting this makes life. Then I wonder, How exciting was lying in that hospital bed all day? How will I explain this to the kids at school?

I feel even stranger when I discover a plastic plunger from a syringe on my desk the following day. Seeing the plastic plunger is scary since I don't recall getting an injection. I'm in disbelief that this even happened until I realize that my left arm hurts, which must be due to the injection. Not remembering any of this makes it complicated for me to ask anyone about it. I want to wash away this whole scary episode. I slather my hair with shampoo in the shower downstairs, even while my head still feels shaky. My face looks out of proportion when I look in the mirror.

Ásta is showing me how to knit. I learned from the kids at school that every child in Iceland learns how to knit. They can't believe I don't know how. Ásta suggests that I knit a long purple scarf to send home to my mom. I'm practicing my knitting when Anna comes over for lunch with the kids. Ásta Björk is curious about what happened to me and asks, Where did they sew you? She looks disappointed when I admit I didn't get any stitches.

Ásta won't allow me to walk to Sigga's house to practice piano. She insists on Jón taking me. She warns me, You can't play for two hours like you usually do.

I follow Ásta's instructions and cut back on my practice time. I'm back in my bedroom working on my knitting when the doorbell rings. Stefania from my class is at the door, plus Juliana, Guðrún, and two other girls whose names I still don't know. They ask how I'm doing. I wonder how they knew I was in the hospital. Oh yes, news travels fast here.

I offer chocolates from the box Ásta gave me and ask them what they did in school yesterday. But then I remember it was a holiday, so they didn't have school. I'm fresh home from the hospital and still light-headed, yet I offer to teach them some easy folk dances like Mayim, an Israeli folk dance, and Salty Dog Rag, an American folk dance. I've brought some record singles from Wisconsin and play them on Ásta and Jón's record player in the living room. The girls catch on quickly. They give me a gift of handcrafted miniatures representing old-style Icelandic farm tools, including a butter churner, a milk bucket, a drinking mug, and a wool spool. Once they leave, Ásta tells me, I knew they would visit. That's how Icelanders are.

In the morning, I feel lethargic and struggle to get out of bed. In typing class, we're supposed to complete a form. The instructions are even more confusing to me than usual. I just type the Icelandic words without knowing what I'm typing. Pálmi asks me, What happened to you with the basketball? I'm too embarrassed to explain when all I know is I was hit in the head by a basketball and ended up in the hospital. I still don't know the precise diagnosis. I invent an imaginary news headline: Wisconsin girl hospitalized in Iceland from watching basketball.

At home for lunch, I'm confused when Ásta shows me three hand-knit Icelandic wool sweaters. We had talked earlier about my wanting to send one home as a birthday gift to my friend Laura, only I don't know the cost. She seems to want me to decide immediately. Finally, I select the one with what I think is the prettiest pattern. Ásta tells me that I can pay later.

I don't feel like myself since the basketball incident. As I watch an Icelandic game show on TV, I reflect on my stay so far. In less than two months, I've partially learned a new language, struggled through fifth-year bookkeeping in Icelandic, and went lame from the wrong size ice skates. Now I've ended up in the hospital from attending a basketball tournament. I can only imagine what lies ahead.

———◇———

Having minimal Icelandic skills made it difficult to bond with friends or participate in social activities. I tried hard to mimic those around me, attempting to ice skate like them, dress more like them, adapt to new types of foods, and even join in Icelandic songs and dances. Later in life, these experiences have taught me how to help others not feel so much like outsiders by assisting foreign students and serving as an English language partner.

My basketball black-out was one of the most traumatic incidents during my stay. I'd only been in the country a few months, wasn't that familiar with the language, hadn't made close friends, and was trying to fit in. I thought going to the basketball tournament was a way to join in school activities with my classmates. I realize now that if I hadn't been standing in that particular spot, it would have been someone else who was injured by the basketball, as the facility did not have enough space for so many spectators.

I felt in the dark from the incident, waking up in the hospital without any explanation that I had a concussion. It was a health scare for my host family, yet I never learned the diagnosis. My parents informed me of this much later in a letter to me. I still don't know how the hospital expenses were paid. It was such an unlikely and strange occurrence. It remains the one time I've ever been hospitalized.

The incident led me to look out more for my safety and comfort. It also added to my sense of claustrophobia of being stuck in crowds and tight spaces. It was early in my stay before I had closely bonded with my host family, and I didn't have my parents to care for me and help me recover. Being primarily on my own through the ordeal helped me become more independent and self-sufficient.

From the ice-skating incident, I learned to wear the right size ice skates and to stop exercising when I experience pain. The basketball incident taught me to avoid large crowds and uncomfortable situations, remain adventurous, and enjoy sports. Following these incidents, I did go on to become an enthusiastic ice-skater, but not a big basketball fan.

WINTER/VETUR 1977-78

———— ◇ ————

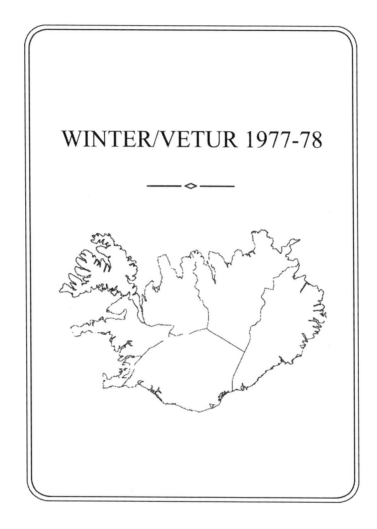

CHAPTER 5

Christmas in Iceland

"Tíu dropar."
Literal meaning: Ten drops.
Intended meaning: Providing impressive hospitality to your visitors, such as your last ten drops of coffee.

Today's my final day of school in Borgarnes. The sun rises much later now and sets earlier. The darkness fools me as to what time of day it is and makes it difficult to get up in the morning. As soon as I drag myself out of bed, I write a dozen Christmas cards to send home and then go to the kitchen for orange juice and a banana. Ásta frowns since she doesn't think it's enough for breakfast.

During Icelandic class, I daydream about traveling around the country while the teacher reads aloud from the *Laxdæla Saga*. I can't believe Christmas break is about to begin, and we still haven't finished this book. So far, I know it's a saga about love and vengeance, but I don't know the ending. In English class, the teacher tells us, It's customary to play games during the last class before break. Two students carry in a stereo system so we can listen to loud music.

In bookkeeping, one final time, I fear we'll have to work on the dreaded fifth-year assignments. Instead, the teacher divides the class into boys and girls and asks quiz questions such as the names of the presidents of Israel, Finland, Sweden, and the United States. The difficulty for me is not only in interpreting the Icelandic but also in trying to decipher his soft voice. When we finish the quiz, the students shuffle the desks and chairs around to create a new seating arrangement. Then we listen to even louder music. Finally, we're free to leave. I run down the school steps feeling liberated from bookkeeping, running to the house in delight with snowflakes falling lightly on my eyelashes.

When I get back to the house, I discover a large package has arrived from my family. It's full of Christmas gifts for me and my host family. Ásta is very curious and she peers into my room just as I'm emptying the contents of the Christmas stocking they sent. In the very tip of the toe, I find a tiny, bruised potato. This is a St. Nicholas Czech tradition (my heritage) placed there as a punishment for any naughtiness during the year. It's hilarious to hear Ásta and Jón argue over who will get to eat the American potato which is barely any larger than the ones grown here in Iceland.

I'm learning that an important element of Christmas celebrations in Iceland is making fancy homemade food. Ásta and I need to start baking as the whole family will be visiting. Since my parents sent a cookbook full of cookie recipes, we will bake as many types of cookies as possible in preparation for Christmas.

I've never baked so much before in my life. It's fun to have an activity that Ásta and I can share without too many glitches in the language barrier. We reap the pleasure of tasting the finished products and receive compliments from the recipients. The difficulty is in converting the measurements to metric. We make a chocolate cake with chocolate frosting and cake rolls with strawberry filling. For Ásta Margrét's upcoming birthday, we make a heart-shaped lemon cake with a lemon filling.

Ásta hands me a sample slice of her delicious homemade white bread. The radio announcer confirms that today is the winter solstice, the shortest day of the year. I'd like to go outside to take photos to document the day. In the rain, I walk down the wet and muddy street to the post office to mail the latest Christmas cards I've written. I climb the forty-nine stairs up to the school, finding it impossible to take a photo when all I see is darkness.

When I enter the kitchen, Ásta greets me with a warm slice of the *rúgbrauð* (dark rye bread) she's just made, fresh out of the can she baked it in. The bread is so moist and delicious that I ask her for the recipe.

I hadn't heard of marzipan before coming to Iceland. The picture of colorful, fun-shaped cookies inspires me to make them. Alone in the kitchen, I make a batch of marzipan cookies in the shape of bananas, apples, oranges, and peapods. Ásta calls me over to the window to look at the sunset after only four hours of dim daylight. The rain has cleared and now the sky is beaming in solid hues of orange, pink, and yellow. Once I photograph the sunset, Jón tells me, The marzipan cookies are so bright and colorful, you should take a photo of them as well. So, I do.

Ásta and I mix up more cookie dough for a batch of chocolate sandwich cookies. Then we mix up yet another recipe for date-filled cookies. While both batches of cookies are in the oven, we watch a rerun episode of *Rich Man, Poor Man* on TV. I'd forgotten this part of the story. I've seen it before, but the soppy, sad story still makes me cry. Then we return to the kitchen to insert the crème filling into the cookies. Jón samples one of the date-filled cookies and says, It tastes so good, you'll have to stay longer! Ásta and I stand in the tiny pantry of the kitchen, counting the filled tins to discover we've made eighteen varieties.

Baking all these cookies with Ásta has made me even closer to her. It's truly extraordinary how quickly she opened her arms to me and has made me feel loved and welcomed. I realize how similar she is to my own mom. Both are great worriers. They find a topic and worry habitually about it until the event has occurred or the issue is resolved. For all their worrying, both are eternal optimists, always looking toward the best outcome. I feel so lucky to have Ásta as my host mother. In addition to my perseverance, she is the main reason

I've learned so much Icelandic. Her love and friendship have helped me manage my homesickness.

I'm halfway home from practicing the piano over at Sigga's when I see Bubbi, who gives me a ride the rest of the way. Bubbi stays for *kaffi* while Ásta suggests that I make my mom's nutmeg feather cake recipe that I've raved about. When the cake is baking in the oven, I write one more Christmas card until Ásta calls me to the kitchen to take the cake out of the oven. We talk excitedly about the upcoming Christmas festivities until bedtime.

As well as baking, I'm discovering how vital visiting is during Christmas time. Sigga's daughter, Ágústa, picks me up in the afternoon to drive me to her friend's farmhouse on the outskirts of Borgarnes. It's blistery cold inside her jeep without any heat. I'm warmed by the landscape's colorful sky in pastel hues. When we enter the farmhouse, we're bombarded by at least ten kids of varying ages, running in every direction. Kids' toys and clothes are strewn about. I smell a strong farm odor, even inside the house. Agústa's friend leads us to the barn to introduce us to the cows and the bull. She tells me the parents own over a hundred sheep, ten horses, and fifteen cows that they milk by hand.

We return to the chaotic household to sip on coffee, snack on Christmas cookies, and watch an Icelandic TV program on how to make Christmas decorations. I'm delighted when one of the young boys chooses to sit in my lap. I learn from Ágústa that we're waiting until five-thirty to watch the milking. The mother asks me in Icelandic, How do you like being here in Iceland? Is it lonely? Do you want to go home for Christmas?

I'm so used to telling people how much I like it here that it doesn't occur to me to answer any differently.

They start the hand-milking of the cows, and I'm shown how to do it. When I try, I discover that milking a cow is more complicated than it looks. I'm delighted when I succeed in squeezing the udder correctly as the milk comes squirting out into the bucket. I laugh as I invent a news headline for today's activity: Wisconsin dairy state girl milks her first cow in Iceland.

Before we leave, the parents ask me to sign their guest book, an Icelandic tradition. The drive home in the heatless jeep is even colder than on the way. I loan my mittens to Ágústa since she needs them more than me to keep her hands warm while driving. We sing Christmas songs together to stay warm on the drive. I help Ágústa with the lyrics in English, and she helps me with the ones in Icelandic.

When Ásta, Jón, and I return to the house from grocery shopping, a girl named Jóhanna is at the door for me. I'm not sure how Ásta and Jón know her. All I know is that they invited her over to visit me. Jóhanna chats with me until Ásta comes to scold me for not inviting my guest to *kaffi*. Ásta sets out a selection of our homemade Christmas cookies for Jóhanna to sample.

During *kaffi*, I've become the "her" in the conversation, as though I'm not in the room. Because Jóhanna lives in the Bifröst area, Jón asks her, What do you think about *Pála* attending Bifröst?

Jóhanna shrugs her shoulders in response.

Jón says, I think it'll be good for her to go to Bifröst since she'll meet students from all over the country. They may be more open rather than the tight-knit group here in Borgarnes.

My hope is that it will be better and that sometime soon, it will be "me" rather than "she" in the conversation.

I walk with Jóhanna to the house where she's staying in Borgarnes. We chat along the way about minorities, languages, drugs, and abortion. Jóhanna describes her year as an exchange student in the United States and how people asked her such silly questions that she gave them sarcastic answers in response. For example, when they asked her how cold it is in Iceland, she'd tell them, Icelanders drink a glass of whiskey a day, so they don't freeze. Jóhanna and I talk about how Icelanders spend all month preparing for Christmas.

I'm lucky that socializing is a priority at Christmas since this is keeping me busy and is helping me fit in better. I'm headed to the Christmas school play and dance, so I dress in my brown, black, and white knee-length print dress with a black turtleneck underneath for warmth. When Ásta sees me in my dressy attire, she says, You look fine! I run through the slippery, snow-lined street and arrive just before the play is to begin. I hand Íris, Hrönn, and Stefania each a small Christmas gift. In return, they each give me an Icelandic kiss on the lips. They hold their packages gingerly, and I wonder what they'll think when they open their gifts to discover a pair of socks. The socks were sent to me by my parents, the only generic enough gift I could think of to give every student in my class.

The little kids in the play are adorable, all dressed up like sheep. When the play is finished, Íris, Hrönn, and I run around outside, arm in arm, with our hair blowing in the wind. We head to the building across from the school, and when we arrive, my sandals and nylons are soaking wet from running through the snow. I hand out the wrapped socks to Pálmi, Óli, and the rest of the boys from my class, and then Juliana, Anna, and I are assigned to collect coats. Kids keep returning for items they've forgotten from their coat pockets. We laugh as we attempt to identify which coat is theirs.

When we finish checking in all the coats, we join the rest of the students on the dance floor. Stefania asks me to dance, and I join her while the song, *I saw Mommy Kissing Santa Claus* is playing, a popular song in Iceland this season. Off and on, students come over to ask me, *Gaman?* This is a noticeable improvement from all the previous days at school when students seemed afraid to talk to me. Now that I've finally broken through the ice and am beginning to fit in, I'm to be sent away.

I'm required to attend periodic Rotary meetings as part of my exchange student responsibilities. For this evening's Rotary Christmas event, the wives aren't invited, which means I'm the only female in attendance and at least fifteen years younger than any of the members. The speeches are dull when I barely understand a word. My consolation is that everyone seems to think the speeches are boring.

As soon as we return to the house, a car pulls up at Ásta and Jón's. Hrönn from school has come to invite me to a scout meeting. I run inside to change into jeans and then leave with Hrönn and her mom. We're driven to the tiny building I've walked past a hundred times and imagined was a model summer cottage. Instead, it turns out to be the meeting place for the Scout Club.

Inside, Pálmi looks at me and asks, Well, is that *Pála*? I count nine candles of various sizes lit on the table. The candles create a cozy atmosphere. Two scouts play their guitars while everyone sings along except me since I don't know the lyrics. It's comforting when we sing a few I know in English. The scouts have brought gifts, and we each pick a number to see which one we'll receive. Mine is a miniature plastic race car.

I'm pleased to discover that Svandís, Birgir, and the kids have arrived. After planting Icelandic kisses on their lips, Birgir Jón is delighted when I present him with the miniature car I received at the scout meeting. We decorate the Christmas tree downstairs, and Jón tries to keep it intact as he moves it upstairs. Once the tree is installed in the living room, we add two more sets of lights and more strands of tinsel. We add so much angel hair that it looks like it's covered in spider webs.

Svandís comes to my room to find me writing in my journal. I compliment her on how thin she looks. She tells me, I've been working on it. All I had for lunch was an apple!

At midnight, the kids are still up, running all over the house, excited about the prospect of opening gifts the next day. The best present I can think of is another letter from home before the post office closes for Christmas.

Christmas Eve morning has arrived. I'm learning that, at least for my host family, this is the biggest day of celebration in the multi-day Icelandic Christmas. Everyone is excited since we will eat special foods, read good books, and exchange presents.

I'm trying to figure out what to wear today since Svandís told me the family dresses up. I'm unsure if they do this right in the morning, so I take a shower and wear my red velour bathrobe out into the hallway to check what the others are wearing. I see Svandís has jeans on, meaning they don't dress up until later. I put on my casual rust-colored corduroy suit, and then Ásta asks me what I'll wear tonight, so I show her my baby blue rug skirt.

While I've always enjoyed dressing up and creating new outfits, I've become even more fashion-conscious here. With the high cost of clothing, Icelanders focus more on quality than quantity when it comes to fashion. My host family and students at school have very well-made, fashionable clothes. They frequently wear the same out-fit several days in a row. This contrasts with my habit of changing outfits frequently, sometimes several times a day. I've been paying attention to how Icelanders put their outfits together. Ásta and Jón bought me a pair of black Icelandic leather clogs like the students here wear. I've added Icelandic wool sweaters to top off my outfits. At home in Wisconsin, I've been allergic to wool. Outside in the cold Icelandic wind, the wool keeps me warm without making me itch or sneeze.

Ásta explains another Icelandic Christmas tradition, the story of *Grýla* (Growler). She tells me, Unlike an American Santa Claus who brings Christmas presents, Iceland has a Christmas Witch, Grýla. She is a scary ogress who punishes naughty children. According to the legend, Grýla has 13 sons, Yule Lads, who live in the mountains. The Yule Lads' job is to steal food and scare children who misbehave.

When Birgir Jón and Linda Björg run around and try to peak at the gifts under the tree, Ásta Margrét admonishes them and tells them, Be good, or Grýla is going to get you! The kids don't seem worried and giggle in delight.

Ásta asks me to bake my mom's nutmeg feather cake again, so I begin making the caramel filling and then the buttercream frosting. The kids have rice pudding for lunch, while the adults eat only apple slices in preparation for the dinner feast. Everyone is sitting in the living room reading. The adults seem to be enjoying the holiday spirit just as much as the kids. Svandís comes into my room and says, I'm so excited for everyone to open presents!

Then I hear a knock at the front door. It's Óli, one of the boys from school wearing his handsome navy-blue double-breasted pea-coat. I see Pálmi and two others I don't recognize, out in the jeep. Óli is carrying a huge package. He explains, It's from the whole class. I give him an Icelandic kiss as he hands me the gift.

When he's gone, Svandís rushes to my room and asks, Who was that handsome boy? Birgir comes to ask the same question. Then Ásta enters my room, smiling, and hands me another huge package.

She tells me, It's from the Borgarnes Rotarians. See, Icelanders aren't so closed. They're really very good!

I'll have to wait until dinner is over to open these packages.

Ásta prepares a Christmas specialty—ten small Icelandic ptarmigans for dinner. I go with Jón to the store to check on his lottery ticket. He discovers he's won a tiny toy car, like the one I won last evening at the scout meeting. In the kitchen, I cut the avocado that Ásta was so excited to purchase since no one here has ever tried one. Meanwhile, everyone samples a slice. Ásta and Svandís both think it tastes good. Ásta Margrét and Birgir's mom don't care for it. I show Ásta how to set the avocado seed in water to let it grow.

Now I'm dressed in my Christmas Eve outfit, a white cotton top with my rug skirt, and I join the others out in the living room. Ásta Margrét looks festive in her new black velvet jumper with pockets. She's acting coy, telling me she already knows what my gift is from my schoolmates. She tells me, It's really neat!

Birgir Jón sits beside me while I read a book in the living room. He's slurping a glass of orange soda with a large spoon, spilling most of it before it reaches his mouth. Svandís starts going around the room Icelandic kissing everyone and wishing them a Merry Christmas, and then Birgir's mom does the same.

I'm wondering if this is an Icelandic custom. When everyone follows suit, I know that it is. We set out the good china and silver and all the food on the dining room table before everyone sits down. The first course is fish, and just when I'm about to put a spoonful of salmon salad in my mouth, Ásta asks, Is it good? I swallow the spoonful before I tell her, It tastes delicious. The famous Icelandic ptarmigan follows the fish. The taste reminds me of the grouse my dad hunts and I've enjoyed at home. When dinner is finished, everyone says they're too full for dessert and won't have it until after the gift opening.

The kids run to the living room to open one present each. Ásta and Jón tell me to do the same, so I open a gift from my classmate Hrönn. I'm delighted to find a pair of hand-knit Icelandic wool mittens inside the package. When all the kids have each opened one gift, we stop to clear the table and wash the dishes. This doesn't take long, with so many to help.

Birgir asks Ásta Margrét and me to hand out the rest of the gifts. I can tell the kids view this role as a privilege, so I attempt to do it with grace and honor.

I'm delighted with the gifts I receive. Ásta and Jón give me a pair of brown sheepskin mittens and a matching sheepskin hat, plus Estée Lauder facial cream like Ásta's. From my classmates, I receive an Icelandic folk music album plus a book of Icelandic verses. From the Borgarnes Rotary Club, a white striped Icelandic wool jacket and, from Anna and Bubbi, a hand-knit button-up Icelandic wool sweater. I don't have to pretend I like the gifts since they're all perfect.

The T-shirt I gave Vigfus is several sizes too big for him. I tell him, You can save it to wear later or give it to someone else. Vigfus immediately becomes so attached to the oversized shirt that he won't give it up. They must not use placemats here since Ásta doesn't know how to use the ones I've given her. The turtlenecks my parents sent for Birgir, Bubbi, and Jón are just the right sizes and colors and they all put them on immediately and are wearing them proudly. Ásta Margrét receives new boots and gray mittens like the ones I was given in brown, Birgir a wool hat similar to mine, and Jón a pair of binoculars and a digital watch. I show them the footed pajamas my parents sent me to stay warm. Ásta Margrét can't believe they are for an adult. She asks, You mean you sleep in this?

Following the excitement of gift opening, Svandís drives Ásta Margrét, Ásta, Jón, and me, over to Anna and Bubbi's. They are pleased to see me wearing the new Icelandic wool sweater they gave me and each give me a big hug. We're offered ice cream, soda, and chocolates, and we talk together until midnight. When we return to Ásta and Jón's, we sample the nutmeg feather cake I made and play the new Icelandic record from my schoolmates. Everyone keeps asking me, Isn't this a wonderful Christmas Eve? I say, *Alveg* (quite), in agreement.

It's Christmas Day, with the emphasis on relaxing together as a family, and we all sleep in late. When I finally get up at eleven, I put on my blue dress pants and a white cotton blouse decorated with bright embroidered birds. Ásta is wearing a green dress with the new copper necklace I gave her from Montana. We have coffee as soon as everyone's awake. The gift opening is done, and the day is a little more laid back, with "fine food" still the emphasis. We set out all the china teacups and the eighteen different kinds of cookies. We drink hot chocolate out of the teacups, topped with tiny marshmallows sent by my parents. Birgir's mom samples the homemade cookies and says, How amazing that a sixteen-year-old could bake all of these! I thank her and acknowledge that I couldn't have done it without Ásta's help.

Svandís and family put on their dress coats, so I put on my new Icelandic wool jacket. We walk in the snow-lined streets without any cars in sight. Clumps of snowflakes blow fiercely across our faces. The slippery road makes it difficult for Svandís to walk in her high-heeled boots. The shops and businesses are closed for Christmas Day, and all is quiet. As we head back to the house, the snowfall gets heavier, with the largest snowflakes I've ever seen.

Anna, Bubbi, and the kids arrive with their slide projector so that the whole family can watch my slides of the United States. Everyone's done with *kaffi* when I've prepared the slides. Since my family has spent several summers at Flathead Lake in Montana, I've included several slides from that area. Anna tells me she's sold on Montana since she thinks the Montana parks, forests, and mountains are the most enticing. As I'm explaining the slides, an exciting climax to my Icelandic language learning is when I realize that I'm no longer translating all words directly from English into Icelandic. This triumph is like another Christmas present.

I have a good laugh when I go downstairs to get the ice cream for Ásta and discover that Birgir Jón has placed his new miniature toy car inside the freezer. I get such a kick out of playing with the kids. I enjoy using my Icelandic with the youngest kids since my language limitations don't interfere with their having fun. I run around with them and swing them around. My parents sent me a candy called Pop Rocks, and the kids giggle in delight when they sample it and feel the candy crystals bubbling and popping inside their mouths. They keep coming to my room to ask for more.

At one in the morning, the adults are in the kitchen drinking brandy, which I sample for the first time. I don't care for the strong alcohol flavor, but I like the sweetness. Birgir says, Jón was worried you would want to attend church while you were here. Lucky for us, you're not religious. I say, I'm also relieved not to have to spend Christmas in church.

Today is the Second Day of Christmas, which is still a formal holiday in Iceland. After so much rich food and celebrating, this is the day to kick back and relax. I sleep in again until eleven, wash my hair, take forever to decide what to wear, and end up dressing in my comfiest and warmest clothes. Today is Ásta Margrét's birthday. I frost the heart-shaped cake I made for her, and she enters the house with her arms full of birthday gifts.

I'm anxiously awaiting my parents' telephone call. As reading books is a big part of the Christmas tradition, Jón, Svandís, and I sit reading on the living room couches. Ásta is talking on a cassette tape to send to Árni in Illinois. The kids listen to a Christmas story on the radio and play with their new toys. I read on as good smells come from the kitchen. Now it's six in the evening, and still no phone call from my family. To avoid disappointment, I try to accept that they may not call.

When the phone rings an hour later, Svandís raises her eyebrows and says with a sigh of relief, *Já* (yes). My heart starts pounding. Jón calls out my name. Then I run to pick up the receiver, Hello?

First, I hear dad's voice, and tears start rolling down my face. I can barely speak since I'm crying so much.

Dad says, We're so happy to get your letters. How can you write so much? How do you have time? Mom can't talk right now since she's crying too much.

We're all very emotional as this is my first phone call with my family since I arrived in Iceland. My sister Dana comes on. I'm crying so hard that I can't get the words out. I made a list of things I wanted to tell them, only my list is in the other room. I tell her about my new Icelandic wool sweaters, and she describes her new, short haircut.

Mom comes back on the line. It's difficult to recognize her voice since she's been crying. She asks, When are you going to *Byfrest*? (her attempt to pronounce *Bifröst*). Are you happy about going there? Did you decide about going to Europe? You should come home soon.

When I tell her that Ásta and Jón were fighting over who would get to eat the tiny, bruised potato she put in my stocking, she tells me if she had known, she would have included a much better, larger one.

Dad pipes in, We opened your package and took a picture with everyone wearing the Icelandic wool scarves you sent. Your sister Robin is crying too hard to come to the phone. If you see a girl named Paula, tell her everyone misses her.

Mom has regained her composure and asks, Is everyone eating the cookies you and Ásta baked? Did they turn out well?

I begin to say *Afskaplega gott* (extremely good). Then I force myself to switch to English. I realize I've answered their questions with the Icelandic *já* instead of an English *yes*.

We are all crying together by then, and I say, Tell everyone how much I miss them and think of them and thanks for calling, thanks for the letters, goodbye.

We hang up and I think about how close they sounded and how vividly I can picture them. Then the missing hits me more than ever, and tears rush down my face. Ásta comes into my room to hug me. I try to translate what my family said. I read the list I made in my notebook and realize I'd forgotten all the questions I'd written down. I'm stuck with a headache from crying so much, and I feel guilty that my family is worried about me when I have it so good.

I wake up at Svandís and Birgir's apartment on the morning of New Year's Eve, having arrived by car with Ásta and Jón the night before. Svandís and I decide to eat only an apple for lunch to prepare for the big dinner this evening. Partial fasting doesn't do any good, since when we visit Svandís' friend Nina, she serves us *kaffi* with a chocolate cake and another cake with strawberry cream filling.

Svandís is excited about roasting a turkey for dinner. She's making it in my honor since she's seen it in American movies. I'm helping her as we follow my mom's turkey stuffing recipe. I laugh when Svandís says, I didn't know you *ate* the stuffing. She thought it was just to add flavor to the turkey. The kids call the turkey "chicken" since they've never eaten it before.

We are preparing a shrimp salad in addition to the turkey and stuffing. I shell the shrimp while Svandís bastes the turkey. Svandís wants to display the whole roasted turkey on a platter at the dinner table, just like in the movies. I convince her that it would be easier to slice the turkey in the kitchen before serving it.

The kids have already begun setting off fireworks out on the balcony. Now everyone gets dressed up for dinner. I put on a black dress with red roses that my sister Robin loaned me. Everyone likes the turkey. Ásta Margrét doesn't like the stuffing because it turned out soggy from cooking it inside the turkey. When we've all had our fill, I join Birgir Jón and Vigfus out on the balcony to light sparklers. In the distance, we can see a big bonfire with bright pink, green, and white fireworks shooting up in the sky. Birgir comes out on the balcony to set off some larger firecrackers. They make loud popping noises as they shoot up high in the sky. The kids want to know if we have fireworks like this in Wisconsin for New Year's Eve. I explain that we usually have fireworks on the Fourth of July. Svandís finds it hard to believe that it would be dark enough. She is used to the twenty-four-hour daylight here in July.

It's cold standing out on the balcony, with giant snowflakes coming down. I don't mind the cold since I'm excited to see all the colorful fireworks. We sample the homemade ice cream that Ásta made this afternoon. It's rich and creamy, almost like frozen whipped cream. We watch a circus program on TV until I notice all the adults have left except Ásta. I ask her where they've gone. She tells me they went to purchase champagne.

We return to the balcony to set off more firecrackers and then run inside at midnight to watch 1977 dim out on the TV screen, and then

1978 shows up in bright colors. Everyone goes around the room saying to each person, *Takk fyrir síðast og gleðilegt nýtt ár* (Thanks for the last and happy new year).

We're all sipping champagne, which I've never tried before. If I gulp it down fast, it doesn't taste too bad. The champagne is followed by a glass of whiskey with Coke as we snack on nuts. It's one in the morning and I'm thinking about going to bed. Instead, I follow everyone downstairs to the neighbor's apartment to snack on pretzels, crackers, and chocolate caramels. The doorbell is constantly ringing as more neighbors stop by to wish everyone a happy new year and to say thanks for the last one.

The neighbors tell me how energetic I am to learn Icelandic. Then pieces of paper are handed around and each person must draw a picture of themselves, blindfolded. Mine looks more like a cartoon character. When I think I can't eat another bite, the table is set with more treats. As we say goodnight and leave the neighbor's apartment at three o'clock, we repeat the same lines, Thanks for the last and happy new year.

In the morning, it feels strange to write 1978 in my journal. Happy New Year's Day everyone, and thanks for the last! Breakfast is hot chocolate, with yesterday's shrimp salad spread on bread and leftover cookies. I feel I'm going to burst from all this eating. Since the weather is snowy white and sublime outside, I take a long walk out to the lighthouse. I wouldn't have thought the weather could be this bright, clear, and picture-perfect before coming to Iceland, with the snow-topped roofs looking like icing dripping down the sides of the houses.

———◇———

The Christmas traditions I learned in Iceland have stuck with me all these years. I continue to go over to anyone who has given me a gift and plant a kiss on their cheek, modified from the Icelandic kiss. Also, making all those cookies using Ásta's super-duper blue Kitchen Aid blender left an impression on me. I continue to be an avid baker, and for my fortieth birthday, my family gave me a super-duper blue Kitchen Aid of my own. Without making all those cookies with Ásta, I might not have taken such an interest in baking. The Christmas holidays were a turning point for me with my newly found capacity to think and dream in Icelandic.

Celebrating Christmas and the New Year in Iceland with all the family activities, learning new traditions and customs, and now having better mastered the language, made me feel more at home and a part of the family. However, other than my host family, I still did not have many close friends to socialize with or confide in. To the credit of Rotary International in the United States, they did check up on my well-being. I recently re-discovered a letter from the Chairman of the Rotary Youth Exchange Program in the United States, who referred to himself as "Grandfather." In his letter to my parents on January 1, 1978, in response to a card I sent to him, he wrote,

We all thought, "Great Caesar, what is this sixteen-year-old child thinking of to choose one of the most barren countries in the world – still with braces on her teeth?" So, now comes this precious Christmas card to Grandfather Harwood from Paula telling of her happiness in her country of adoption. Apparently, we were wrong in worrying about her welfare and stamina to tackle a faraway land like Iceland. When your daughter returns in summer, 1978, she will no longer be a teenager as when she left last September. She will be a mature, intelligent young woman ready to again become a part of her native America and her ongoing education. Her experience in a foreign culture will be invaluable to her.

Reading his letter now, over forty years later, reminds me of the special interest that "Grandfather" Harwood took in my well-being. Also, the Borgarnes Rotary Club did its best to look out for my welfare by inviting me to their meetings and staying updated on my activities through my host father's reports. Each day, I retained a positive outlook, trying to put my best foot forward, always working to make friends and improve my Icelandic.

CHAPTER 6

Boarding Under a Rainbow

"Gera hreint fyrir sínum dyrum."
Literal meaning: Now the knife's stuck in the cow.
Intended meaning: Now you've done it, finding yourself in a difficult situation.

Since Ásta and Jón's son Árni went to live in Antioch, Illinois, it made sense that his parents host a student in his empty bedroom. I think Ásta and Jón have enjoyed my stay and may have even become a little attached to me, as I have to them. I also imagine entertaining a sixteen-year-old who arrived knowing no Icelandic has not been an easy task. With no other families volunteering, Haukur Ingibergsson, the headmaster at the Bifröst School and a Rotarian, has generously offered me a place to stay. His home is a boarding school, meaning I'll live in a dormitory without any actual host family.

Now that the Christmas and New Year's celebrations are over, today, January 5, 1978, is the day I'm supposed to begin my life at Bifröst. I just learned that the school's name has to do with an Old Norse tale about a rainbow bridge of the gods. I hope my stay here will be showered with rainbows followed by golden opportunities.

Jón and I lug my suitcases into the back of his miniature grey work truck. I hold back my tears as I say goodbye to Ásta. We head out on the thirty-kilometer gravel road drive, mostly in silence. Jón has a much quieter demeanor than Ásta. He astounds me with how he has embraced me as if I were his own daughter in such a short time. I admire his lovely sense of humor. His eyes sparkle when he finds something funny, and his whole body jiggles. He reminds me of my dad; pensive, a diligent worker, always looking out for everyone. Even his eyes squint when he smiles, a trait my siblings and I have inherited from my dad. Jón is convinced I will become a journalist since I'm always writing in my journal.

When Jón takes the final turn up the long narrow driveway to the austere-looking boarding school, my heart feels heavy in my chest with a burning sense of fear. The two-story school building stands alone, with no trees to soften its image. The burnt red roof with pale yellow trim around the tiny windows makes me fear I'll feel claustrophobic once inside. The driveway is devoid of cars or any signs of life. I'm comforted by the splendid snow-capped mountains framing the outside of the building.

We find the headmaster in his office tucked several doors beyond the entranceway. Haukur speaks to me in English.

I'm putting you in a room with a girl who is the housemother for the school.

I'm too full of anxiety to ask what that means.

Haukur asks, Do you speak Icelandic?

Only Icelandic. This is the absolute truth, as I have barely spoken English in the past several months.

We haul my heavy suitcases upstairs, and then I say goodbye to Jón. I meet my new "housemother" roommate, Alla Rúna, who is three years older than me. She's wearing a pale blue and white striped dress and stands about five feet tall, super thin, with a petite pug nose, tiny blue eyes hidden under orange tinted spectacles, a freckled face, and shoulder-length, red hair. I'm discovering that the housemother title comes from her role of helping others with their homework and overlooking the welfare of others. Unfortunately, based on her greeting, I don't think this role of assistance extends to me.

Alla Rúna's glare as she watches me unpack makes me think she's unhappy I'm her new roommate. She says, You'll sleep on the top bunk. While I unpack my suitcases into the one empty drawer and the tiny remaining space in the miniature closet, she asks one question, Do you smoke? I reply, No. I'm not pleased to learn that she does, as I soon discover most of the eighty students at this boarding school do.

The school secretary knocks to tell me to return to the headmaster's office to get my class schedule. Haukur explains in Icelandic, This is a different type of school. I'm unsure what he means by this. He hands me a copy of my class schedule, full of bookkeeping and accounting classes.

Haukur leads me downstairs to introduce me to a student named Ágústa, who'll be in my class. My roommate, Alla Rúna, is in the class above me as the school has two levels. I'm assigned to the first class with students closer to my age but, on average, two years older. This is unlike Borgarnes, where I was one of the oldest of my classmates.

Bifröst is a junior college that prepares students for college or university. This means I must get used to a whole new set of classes. Haukur has assigned Ágústa to give me a tour of the school. I notice how inconveniently located the bathroom is, ten rooms away from my room, down the long hallway. Ágústa takes me to the basement level to point out the darkroom for photography, the gym, the lockers, the showers, and the sauna.

Ágústa tells me, All the classes here are difficult for us, so I can imagine how difficult they'll be for you. Her assertion heightens my level of fear. I follow Ágústa and her roommate to the cafeteria for dinner: fish topped with melted cheese and potatoes.

I barely sleep during my first night at Bifröst. The temperature keeps changing from too hot to too cold. Much of the night, I lie awake anticipating the morning wake-up call. A loud banging begins at the opposite end of the hallway. A male student pounds on each door, opens it, and then yells in a robust shout, *Goðan daginn* (Good day)! Since our door is the furthest away from his starting point, I hear the loud banging repeated at each door until he reaches ours.

I can't seem to escape bookkeeping, the first class of the morning. In fact, I've learned that this junior college specializes in business and bookkeeping. At least for today, this class is a slight improvement over the one in Borgarnes since I receive a little help from the teacher.

The boarding school concept is strange to me, with students willingly choosing to live away from their families to study. Since most students here are 18-25 years old, they may be less likely to be as homesick as I am. A few girls from my class admit that they occasionally miss home. One girl tells me how rare it is for her to spend any time at home.

She says, I stay at this school all winter long, and then in the summer months, I work far away from home. I only see my family during the weekends I have off from school or work.

I ask her, When do kids start to work in Iceland?

She replies, I was only eight when I started selling newspapers in my hometown.

In Danish class, one of the male students tells me, If you find the class boring, don't worry, we all find it boring. I look around the room and notice the inattentiveness of the students. One girl is knitting. Another girl leaves to get her transistor radio. I'm daydreaming about my family visiting and how I would translate for them. They should visit while I'm here this year. Otherwise, I might forget my Icelandic.

I'm impressed to learn that the political economics teacher is the author of the book we're using. He has a distinguished professorial look, with white hair and a bald spot on the top of his head, always wearing his brown and white patterned Icelandic wool sweater.

One of the students in my class has a name that sounds like mine, something like "*Páli.*" I suppose it's the Icelandic translation of "Paul." Whenever the student's called on, it sounds like the teacher is saying my name. Páli points out that I need the book the teacher's written, so the teacher loans me one. Although now that I have a book, I still can't guarantee results.

In typing class, I must transition to using an electric typewriter, a big switch from the manual I used in Borgarnes. One day when I arrive in class, the typewriter assigned to me is missing, so the teacher must find a different one for me to use. Then I rip the paper, trying to insert it into the typewriter. I lose my place when I can't understand the words and mistakenly type the same paragraph twice. I make many mistakes trying to type the different Icelandic characters, the *ð*, the *þ*, and the *æ*, and the vowels with umlauts and accents. I continue to doubt typing in Icelandic with a different keyboard is doing me any good. I'll have to learn it all over again when I return to Wisconsin.

A new week is beginning. I tell myself, make it a good one. I remember what a friend told me back home, An exchange student's year is like a V. It's good initially. Halfway through, you take a big dip. Then another rise when it's about time to leave. So far, this seems accurate.

Group dynamics is another "favorite" of mine. Today in class, each student is asked to give a short speech about a school club and how it could be improved in the coming year. I am excluded since I have not participated in any school club, and I won't even be here next year. The exercise reinforces my feeling of being an outsider. We're told to go to our assigned groups. We're supposed to discuss issues about when an individual becomes independent in Iceland at twenty-one. The students are chatting about everything except the topic we're told to discuss.

Since I had a spacious room of my own in Borgarnes, it's challenging to share a tiny room with Alla Rúna. I appreciate how she could be unhappy about my arrival mid-year since she's had the space to herself up until now. She has control over the radio, so no more listening to the Keflavík English station for me. It's the middle of winter and cold outside, and she keeps leaving the window wide open. She has the habit of running the cold sink water over a Coke bottle for several hours so it's chilled when she's ready to drink it. I'm sure I'm not the perfect roommate match. Perhaps I have habits that irritate her, such as my nightly floor exercises and my failure to know the answers to her English assignments. I'm trying to be as friendly and inconspicuous as possible in our tiny, shared space.

Writing in my journal has become my daily lifeline. Guðbjörg (or Gugga for short, pronounced Gūgka) is in the room visiting when she notices me writing.

Gugga says, I wonder if you'll ever read the journals you've been keeping.

I say, Maybe one day you'll be able to go to the store and buy a copy.

Alla Rúna adds, I'd never buy it. That's insane!

To have any social life at this boarding school, I must work hard to make friends. In the lounge area downstairs, I discover a Czech magazine published in English, and I page through it. Þór (pronounced Thor), from my class, looks at my magazine through his long shaggy hair and wire-rimmed glasses. He asks, What are you reading? This initiates a discussion about the difficulties of the Icelandic language. When Ásta and Jón's son, Árni, comes up in the conversation, I discover Þór knows Árni since they're both from Borgarnes. Students keep walking past, giggling to see me engaged in a conversation with a boy. Þór invites me to his room to show me his comic books. He tells me this is how he learned most of his English. That must be why he's such a comic himself!

Þór shows me the photos he's developed in the darkroom and helps me pronounce the students' names in class. Then he invites me to the cafeteria for *kaffi*. I feel sheepish, trailing behind him down the steps and through the hallway. In the cafeteria, I can't think of what to say to him, with another guy sitting directly across from us. I'm still uncomfortable speaking Icelandic in front of more than one person.

Ágústa tells me that dance class is about to begin. I switch into shoes fit for dancing and go to the cafeteria to join the others. All the girls stand on one side of the room and the boys on the other. When the instructor arrives, I'm stunned to see that he is my piano teacher from Borgarnes. He talks slowly, showing each step over and over, first the girls' footwork, then the boys'. I was curious about the kinds of dances he would teach. I'm already familiar with several, like the polka, waltz, and tango. His instructions are painfully slow and straightforward, and the girls must sit down after each new step and wait for the boys to pick a new partner.

Following a short break, the instruction continues with steps that are a little more intricate and fun. One difference I notice is that, unlike the Wisconsin polka, there's no hop in the polka he teaches. As the teacher gives his slow instructions, my mind bursts with thoughts unrelated to the dancing. The reality that I'm stuck at this boarding school out in the middle of nowhere for a semester is starting to sink in. In terms of learning about Icelandic family life and culture, this is not the place for it. When the dance instruction ends at eleven, I dread tomorrow's wake-up call.

Our next extracurricular activity is to visit the nearby Grábrók Crater. When our classes are finished for the day, I follow the students outside to gather a five-foot-high pile of firewood. I help load the firewood into an open trailer attached to the back of a jeep. Then we all climb into the trailer. We're so crammed in on the ride to the crater that I fear I might fall out the back end. My spirits improve when I take in the breathtaking sight of the snowy, mountainous landscape in every direction.

Once the jeep stops, each student picks up a large empty cardboard box and fills it with firewood. Then we begin the steep climb to the top of the 170-meter-high crater rim. The portion of the path covered in snow is more manageable to trudge through than the bare, large, slippery black lava stones. The soles of my boots slip on the black lava, making each step a painful upwards hike. At least this isn't as painful as skating in those killer ice skates.

As we progress slowly up the steep mountainside, the wind blows so fiercely that it threatens to send me straight back down. I have trouble keeping my balance with the heavy load of firewood in my arms. My nose is dripping incessantly. The droplets fly through the wind and slap across my face. I'm afraid the wind will steal my hat as well. Since I didn't know what I was in for, I didn't dress for the frigid weather. The other students look like they're staying warm in their Icelandic wool sweaters, wool coats, and scarves, chatting cheerfully. They're laughing away as they climb upward over the rocky, slippery terrain.

When we reach the top of the crater, the students form an assembly line. The student behind me hands me a heavy load of firewood that I'm supposed to pass to the girl beside me while I struggle to avoid slipping.

Once we've completed what I think is our fair share of moving the heavy firewood, I run down the mountainside with three of the girls, even while one of the students shouts at us, More firewood is on its way! Most of the other students make yet another trip back up the mountain. I wonder where they get their energy.

On the ride back to Bifröst, I struggle to keep my balance as I again stand in the back of the open trailer behind the jeep. We're racing along the dark country road, with the freezing wind blowing on my numb face. I cringe to know that tomorrow night, we must climb back up Grábrók Crater for the bonfire.

Alla Rúna is missing from our dorm room when I get back, giving me some rare moments to myself. Treading through the snow has left the lower half of my jeans soaked through to my skin, and my entire body feels numb. At least now I have a better picture of the landscape surrounding Bifröst. This new vision is not that comforting as it confirms how secluded it is here, with only two buildings besides the school. One is the teachers' housing, and the other is a small, brown house which is Haukur's home.

Dressed in my long winter underwear under my jeans the following evening, I'm attempting to be better prepared for another challenging climb up the mountain. When we arrive at the bottom of Grábrók, we're each given a long pole with a gasoline-soaked rag attached to the end, which is then lit. As we climb the mountainside, a scary image forms in my mind of the Ku Klux Klan, all in single file, holding our lit torches. My entire body is shaking from the cold, so I wrap my scarf around my neck and tuck the ends inside my jacket. Then my neck gets soaking wet with sweat.

At the top, students use their torches to light the bonfire. The bright, flaming fire framing the top of Grábrók Crater is a spectacular sight. When two of the students set off some fireworks, I think this cold, achy feeling might be worth it, even when I'm still unsteady on the steep mountaintop, constantly slipping either backward or forward. Going down the mountain is more challenging than going up since we no longer have our torches to see in the dark. Several students give up on walking down and slide down on their butts the rest of the way.

When I reach the bottom, I discover we won't receive a ride back this time, and we start the long, cold walk back to the school. Eventually, I end up walking faster than the rest of the group. Walking alone on the road in the pitch dark is scary until I catch up to two girls. I'm not sure of their names, but I enjoy their company.

One of the girls breaks the silence by asking me, What's your name? How do you like Bifröst? I tell her it's fun, although the cold has diminished my language ability, making me feel like I'm speaking baby talk. Then I remember one of the second-year students who recently asked me how many *years* I've lived in Iceland, and I cheer up.

Today we have a bus ride to another school event, some type of multi-school dance. The students pile onto the bus. The bus ride lasts an hour, and then I follow the others into a building, unsure where we are. Once inside, I see the Borgarnes bookkeeping teacher and Pálmi, Hrönn, and Íris from my Borgarnes class, plus some of the students I met at the Hvanneyri school. Several ask how I like Bifröst. I respond with the expected niceties.

The entertainment is about to begin, and I learn that this event is a meeting of students from four schools. Now that I've lived in Iceland for five months, I recognize most of the students here, and they know me, if not by name, by face. This is because I've had connections with all four schools: by attending the school in Borgarnes, then visiting Hvanneyri plus meeting the Varmaland girls at the dances, and finally by attending Bifröst. The ones from Borgarnes knew me the longest, and they are the friendliest, coming up to say hello and asking me how it's going at Bifröst.

A set of skits by students from each school precedes the dance. While mostly amateurish, some of the performers are pretty talented. I'm impressed with the dance performance by a girl from my Borgarnes gym class to the Carole King song, *I Feel the Earth Move*. I can't imagine anyone performing this back home without receiving a lot of wisecracks about the skimpy outfit. Her dance movements and choreography show promise.

Then the girls from Bifröst sing a song, wearing no pants, only black shirts with underwear and black nylons. In another skit, several students hold up a blanket while a guy and girl throw their clothes over the blanket from behind. They make loud groans as if they're having sex. When the students drop the blanket, they reveal that the guy and girl are cleaning a cupboard. I wonder if they'd allow these kinds of skits at my high school.

Finally, the dance begins, and a second-year boy from Bifröst asks me to dance. We dance the polka together, without much space. My black Icelandic clogs are tight in the toes, making it painful whenever someone steps on them.

I notice that students from each of the different schools are congregating at separate tables. Under other conditions, I might have been sitting at the Borgarnes or the Hvanneyri table.

We board the bus to leave at two in the morning. The bus ride back seems to take longer than on the way there. As we cross a bridge, it feels like the bus is going about five kilometers an hour with only three inches of leeway between the bus and the side. Looking down at the deep drop into the river in the early morning reminds me of how far away I am from Wisconsin. It suddenly strikes me how unusual it is for me to be on a bus in Iceland, full of Icelanders, singing Icelandic songs.

Little do I know what is in store for me the following evening. Alla Rúna tells me there's a movie showing at six this evening. I head downstairs to purchase a bag of popcorn and a Coke from the school canteen to enjoy during the film in the library. Then to my astonishment, the students begin rolling a movie called *The Ladies Journal*, with the lead woman, who looks about 60 years old, lying on a bed holding a giant plastic penis, having intercourse with another woman. This is my first exposure to any form of pornography, and I find it shocking. I can't imagine the students getting away with this. Certainly not at my high school.

Today is an Icelandic holiday called *Bolladagur* (Bun Day). One of the second-year students explains that this was originally a Danish tradition that Icelanders have adopted. Children would decorate a stick made of paper to use as a wand to spank their parents while shouting, *bolla, bolla, bolla* (bun, bun, bun)! The parents then re-warded their children with cream buns equal to the number of times their kids managed to spank them. The celebration has evolved into a day devoted to eating delicious cream buns.

Two girls knock on our dorm room door at six-thirty in the morning. We head to the kitchen to prepare trays of cream buns to deliver to the boys. Some of the girls have been awake for several hours getting ready, loading the trays with the baked buns, sliced bread, *hangikjöt* (smoked mutton), and green pea salad. The girls are writing personalized notes to set on each tray.

Alla Rúna informs me that she has changed my room assign-ment. Now, I'm assigned to Room 207. I don't know whose room this is or what I'm to say when I get there. The girls hand me a tray and are astonished that I haven't prepared a note. Fortunately, I learn another girl is to accompany me. We carry our trays upstairs, enter-ing Room 207. When the male students in the room see us with the trays of buns, one says, Oh, today's Bun Day. This is anticlimactic after the long hours and drama that went into creating the perfect trays to deliver.

The girls return to the kitchen, exchanging their stories. some say that the guys were surprised. In our case, they simply weren't that interested. All the girls sit in the cafeteria since it's our turn to eat the remaining fresh baked buns. With relief, I discover no spank-ing occurs during Bun Day at Bifröst. I'm wondering what other celebrations I have yet to learn about here in Iceland and whether this boarding school will live up to its name so I can find happiness at the end of the rainbow.

———◇———

All these years later, I'm thankful I survived my stay at Bifröst. I went to Iceland to learn about the country, the language, the cus-toms, and the family life. I did not picture living in a dormitory in a boarding school without a host family. Instead of additional host families, I received a school stay. The Borgarnes Rotary Club decided it would be yet another educational experience for me, and they were right about that.

I felt like I was in an experiment, with me as a strange fish thrown in with some sharks to see if I could make friends. Despite how lonely it was boarding at Bifröst, it never occurred to me to pack up and return early to Wisconsin. I forced myself to use the new language, even when the students had studied English much longer than I had Icelandic. When I think about how traumatic some of these experiences were, I wonder why I was so adamant about staying the course. I'm proud now to realize how brave I was to persevere at such a young age.

CHAPTER 7

Outside Time for an Outsider

"Gakktu hægt um gleðinnar dyr."
Literal meaning: Walk slowly through the doors of joy.
Intended meaning: When good things happen, don't get too
excited and hurt yourself.

The word *útivist* (outdoors or outdoor activities) has special sig-
nificance at Bifröst. As part of the schedule, a separate time is set
aside each day to spend outside. Something like recess. This is a
little unusual since we're talking about 18 to 25-year-olds, not little
kids. I'm learning the importance *of útivist.* Since we eat, sleep,
and attend classes in the same building, we spend most of the time
cooped up inside. Ironically, *útivist* makes me feel like *less* of an
"outsider" than when I'm inside the school.

With Alla Rúna gone to visit her boyfriend for the weekend,
I'm savoring these precious moments of privacy. Classes are over
for the day, except with the rain and sleet, I won't be able to participate in *útivist.*

I stand at the cafeteria entrance reading the bulletin board when
Þór comes by and asks me if I liked last night's student debate about
the American Air Force base in Keflavik. He says he enjoys meetings
like this since they're good for practicing public speaking. I realize
I might have a slight crush on Þór because it makes me nervous just
talking to him.

To prepare for an alumni performance this evening, I change my earrings, dab on perfume and ChapStick, and fill my pockets with a supply of gum. I glance in the mirror and give myself a pep talk, Come on *Pála*, go down there and face them! On my way downstairs, I meet Ágústa and Íris. I follow them to their room to chat for a while, with other students popping in and out. Having an entire conversation with a group in Icelandic makes me give a silent cheer.

I tag along with Ágústa and Íris to get seats for the evening performance. Former Bifröst students pile in. Íris tells me it's common for former students to return for this type of event. Once all the students have gathered in the cafeteria, the visiting alumni perform several songs and skits. The lyrics to the songs include jokes about the Bifröst teachers. The routine with the guys dressed up like ballerinas gets a good round of laughs.

When the performances are done, I sit on the edge of the lower bunk bed in Ágústa and Íris' room, watching the girls dance to Icelandic rock and roll music. The girls here have a style of dancing that I haven't seen in Wisconsin. They take one small step out to the right and then turn to bump the hip of the girl closest to them. Then they bump their shoulders together, next their feet. It reminds me a little of the bump dance, popular several years ago. This is a unique version. It makes for a funny scene as they dance in long, baggy blouses without bras.

Back in the hall, the floor has been opened for dancing. I have a stomachache and wonder how late this alumni dance will last with the music blaring. I remind myself that I learn more from painful experiences than tolerable ones.

I'm at my desk writing a letter home on Sunday afternoon when Alla Rúna and her boyfriend return. It's uncomfortable with the three of us crowded together in our tiny room. The bell rings, and Alla Rúna tells me it means chorus practice is starting, giving me an excuse to leave. I enter the cafeteria, unsure whether I'm allowed to join in. I gasp a little when I recognize the chorus teacher, the same teacher who taught the dance classes and my piano lessons. I'm handed sheet music for some Icelandic songs and enjoy singing along.

That evening, on a school excursion to the movie theater in Borgarnes, the bus makes its way along the bumpy road, and I realize this is the first time I've been outside in five days. With so much time spent inside, it feels strange going from the bare, pristine landscapes of Bifröst to the familiar houses, buildings, and shops of Borgarnes. Once we arrive at the theater, I discover the movie we'll be seeing is *The Man Who Fell to Earth* with David Bowie. I can't decipher some of the words through the thick British accent. I'm thinking how parents at home would disapprove of a school trip to an X-rated movie. A Bifröst teacher sits in the chair beside me. He tells me, This is my second time seeing this movie. On the return drive to Bifröst, I think what a shame it is to drive the thirty kilometers in the dark and barely get a glimpse of the sky.

Before class on Tuesday morning, Sveinn, the English teacher, asks me if I would show my slides of the United States to the class tomorrow to give the students a break before exams. The opportunity makes me feel less like an outsider. Sveinn comes to the door to check whether I've been able to get the projector to work. I ask him in my best Icelandic, Do you think I'll have a chance to show slides another time as well? He tells me, It depends since this is an extra event, and they already have other field trips planned for future free time.

Once I start showing slides of landscapes, cityscapes, and famous monuments, my nerves calm down. Due to our travels around the United States, I'm lucky my dad and I have taken many slides. The students are so quiet that I fear I've put them to sleep. No one laughs or utters a word. Sveinn asks one impossible question, How much salt is in the Great Salt Lake? I chuckle to myself as I'm expected to be the expert on every aspect of the United States. Following his solitary question, one of the students asks Sveinn when they can leave.

I switch seven slides during the break. I want to catch Sveinn off guard when I give my presentation to the second-year students. When Sveinn sees the new slide of the Texas oil well, he says, Surely, they're bigger than that. No, I tell him, that's the actual size. Showing the slides is more fun this time around since these students are wider awake.

The last class of the day, bookkeeping, is nearing its end. The students are anxious about their exams tomorrow, not knowing which three of the five classes on which they'll be tested. This system forces them to study the material from every class. I've avoided being at Bifröst during past exams by scheduling an orthodontist appointment in Reykjavík. Not this time. A part-time student, Helga, who also won't be taking the exams, will show me how to use the darkroom.

While the others are studying, I head to the darkroom in the basement. When Helga shows up, she tells me, You must pick out the prints you want to make copies of and then find the negatives.

I watch with anticipation as she shows me how to soak the white photo paper in the solution. I carefully select the negatives I want to print and then ask her to check the lighting and tell me how long to wait. This is my first experience working in a darkroom, and it's magical to see the images appear as the photo paper soaks into the solution. I reprint the photos of the Bifröst students and teachers and use clothespins to hang them on the string line to dry.

I'm skipping dinner because I'm engrossed in working in the darkroom. My feet are aching from standing so long, and my eyes are tired of the dark. However, this is one of the magical rainbow moments I was hoping for. When I finish printing copies of all the negatives I selected, I proudly examine the twenty prints I developed myself and think photography might hold something for me in the future.

Thrilled by this magical activity, I decide this is an opportune time to use the sauna while everyone is upstairs studying. A gust of steam comes out when I enter the sauna through the women's shower room. I notice a door on the other side that might lead to the boys' locker room. Luckily, none will come in now since they're all studying.

Sitting on the wooden sauna bench with my eyes closed, I soak up the heat until I hear the opposite door opening. My eyes open quickly to see Óli strolling in with nothing on except a towel. Luckily, I have a towel and quickly wrap it tighter around my body. Another male student enters closely behind Óli, also wearing nothing but a towel and giving me a strange look. This is too uncomfortable. I jump up to leave, with my bare butt peeking out from under my towel as I exit. I wonder, do all the students share the sauna in the nude? I'll never know the answer since this will be my first and last time.

With exams over, students are getting ready to leave for a free weekend. I'm excited to be going to visit Ásta and Jón. When we'd talked on the phone the day before, Ásta had sounded just as excited. She asked lots of questions without giving me a chance to answer.

Are you using the mittens and socks? Yes, you better use them. Plus, you must bring them with you. Oh, and don't forget the quilt and boots. This Saturday night is a dance in Borgarnes, and Birgir and Svandís will be coming. Have you lost weight? Then she tells me about all the good things she'll make for me to eat.

It feels warm and comforting to be in Borgarnes with Ásta and Jón as I show them the photos I developed in the darkroom. Ásta is full of questions about Bifröst, How's the food, how's your roommate, do many kids smoke? She seems as glad as I am that I'll be skipping the school exams next month since I've conveniently scheduled another orthodontist appointment in Reykjavík at that time.

With all the visiting I've done here in Iceland, I've become a bona fide coffee drinker. During *kaffi*, Svandís calls, and I'm pleased to be able to follow most of what Ásta explains to her; how I've lost so much weight, have presents for the kids, and a girl at Bifröst asked me how many *years* I've lived in Iceland.

We watch the news on the TV downstairs, including a story about a big snowstorm in Ohio. We hear Svandís' voice calling us, and we run upstairs to greet Birgir and Svandís with Icelandic kisses. When they compliment me on my Icelandic, I realize how much more comfortable I am with it. They have come to Borgarnes to attend tomorrow evening's Rotary Ball.

Later the next afternoon, Anna and the kids stop to visit. My parents sent coloring books and crayons for me to give to Ásta Björk and Jón Bjarni. We munch on the rice crispy bars I made, which they've never tried before, and say they're delicious. As soon as Bubbi stops to pick up the kids, Ásta tells me to hurry and get ready for the Rotary Ball.

When we enter the Borgarnes Hotel, the mailman comes over to greet me. Practicing his English, he says, If any mail arrives for you tomorrow, I'll bring it to the house for you. He must see the homesickness on my face and is hopeful that I'll receive some more letters. Then Sigga and her two daughters arrive, and Sigga introduces me to a man who is the father of Þórster, a student at Bifröst.

Do you know my son, Þórster?

Já, fint strákur (Yes, nice boy).

My son said the same of you.

Several Rotarians give short speeches while we eat dinner. Ásta tells me, I'll bring some fish to the table for you to taste. She puts a piece on my plate and insists, This is an Icelandic delicacy you will like. When I cut a small piece and put it in my mouth, I'm not sure what to do with it since it's so tough it's impossible to chew or swallow. Now I recognize that this isn't any ordinary fish. It's fermented shark meat, similar to what she had me try at Sigga's house the first month I arrived. The taste is like cold, moldy cheese with a smell of ammonia. I'm thankful that Ásta is willing to take the remaining rubbery piece off my plate.

An older Rotarian Is playing the piano. Ásta claps vigorously, knocking the silverware off the table. Three men start to play instruments and sing while Birgir invites me to dance. Then the mailman asks me to dance, which is embarrassing since he's had too much to drink. I'm even more embarrassed when another Rotarian asks me to dance and repeatedly tells me in English, You're afraid of me. I excuse myself and go upstairs to the bathroom. When I return, I talk with two Rotarians who hold onto my hands, telling me I look much older than sixteen. I suppose this could be a compliment, only it feels a bit threatening.

The Rotary Ball is finally over at three in the morning. Everyone collects their coats. The chilly night air is refreshing compared to the loud music in the crowded, heavily heated room. Ásta, Jón, and I sing Icelandic songs together while we walk back to the house.

Óli arrives the following morning to give me a ride to Bifröst. I wish the drive would go on forever since I'm not anxious to return to my suffocating room. I open the dorm room door to discover Alla Rúna and Gugga sitting and smoking on the lower bunk bed. They each give me a casual, *Hæ*, and then return to their private conversation. I could have gone to the moon and back for all they seem to care.

Monday morning, I learn that Danish class is canceled, so I lie in bed snacking on a banana and reading a book. I'm still concerned about the warning that exchange students tend to gain weight, even while I guiltily eat several of the cookies Ásta sent along with me. Alla Rúna seems delighted when I tell her she can have some of the cookies and she can borrow the cassette tapes I brought along from

Borgarnes. When I turn on one of the cassettes, Alla Rúna tells me, *Alveg frábært* (absolutely great)!

At eleven that evening, Sigrún tells me that all the girls from the first and second-year classes are to congregate in the library for a planning meeting to create a new girls' club. Everyone's dressed in pajamas and bathrobes. Ágústa and Helga are in charge, with Sigrún taking notes. Each member (except me) is invited to the podium to present ideas for new activities. Everyone agrees they want to do something special, like taking a walk together during *útivist*. In one breath, one of the girls suggests that we go on a diet together; in the next breath, others suggest we make pancakes.

We elect Hardís, a second-year student, as the new club leader. The girls decide that we need a name for the club. One of the girls suggests the name *"Grábrók,"* in honor of the nearby crater we've climbed up twice. Although I was invited to join this club, I still feel like an outsider. It doesn't help that I wasn't here for the first half of the year, that I'm much younger than all of the students, and I won't be here next year.

Classes are over the following day, and I'm prepared with my outdoor gear, camera, and chewing gum. I wait with Ágústa and Þórinn until we have a group of ten for *útivist*. Once outside, all ten girls link arms in a line, and we sing as we walk along together. The bright sunshine makes it much warmer than the previous days. We play follow-the-leader, and skip, hop, and sing Icelandic chants that I mimic a little delayed behind the others as they shout them out.

We come to a bridge, and I use this opportunity to take a photo of all the girls lined up across it. Through photography, I'm finding a way to better communicate and express myself creatively. We peek into the windows of a summer house locked up for the season and then cross over an entire lake of ice. We peer through the windows of a small barn to see several fuzzy, wet sheep huddled together inside.

I'm disappointed when only five girls show up for *útivist* the next day until I discover what a fun bunch they are. We cross the road and over a fence and spot several Icelandic horses. They're somewhat smaller than other breeds of horses and are sometimes mistakenly referred to as ponies. They are hearty, sure-footed horses brought to Iceland by the Vikings. We discover one of the horses has escaped from behind the fence, giving us the opportunity to pet its soft light brown fur and long flowing mane. This horse is so affectionate that I receive a welcoming glance responding to my strokes and caresses. We continue trekking through the snow. When I talk with Helga, she compliments me, You're energetic with speaking Icelandic.

When I take a painful fall on the ice, I fear the nick on my knee will turn into a nasty bruise. I don't know how the others can cross the ice so quickly and easily. We walk past huge boulders of ice, and I stop to photograph the icy white landscape mixed with splotches of blue sky behind the white clouds. As we return to the barn and summer house, we look in through the downstairs window and then continue along the road on the other side of Grábrók mountain. I take more photos of the Icelandic horses, with the Bifröst school building off in the distance, as we make our way down the hill.

Studying in my dorm room, three second-year girls knock on my door to ask if I have a "sexy" nightgown they could use for the school play. I remember the pink polka-dotted nightgown my mom told me she wished I would throw out. The girls seem pleased with it. I'm wondering how they'll use it in the play.

I pick up my sheet music and head to chorus practice. Once again, the teacher doesn't show up. We continue rehearsing without him. When I return to my room, Gugga is sitting at my desk chair, so I have nowhere to sit or write. Alla Rúna asks me about an English word for a place where a carpenter works. It seems this should be obvious, but I can't think of it. The perturbed look on her face is as if she's thinking, what good is an English-speaking roommate if she can't even help me with my English assignment?

Only Sigrún and I show up for *útivist* this time. She's interested in practicing her English. Since I've barely spoken a single word of English for months, I'm the one who is reluctant to talk in English. As we walk side by side, we discuss traveling to Europe as Sigrún carries on in English, and I use Icelandic. The wintry weather is numbing my face, causing me to stumble over my words, while Sigrún pokes fun at my pronunciation. Since I'm a visual learner, I find it difficult to say some of the Icelandic words I've learned from only hearing them without having seen them written down.

When we return inside, the first-year girls are in the kitchen mixing up batter for *pönnukökur* (Icelandic pancakes). They use three pans on the stove to fry the pancakes. They fill them with cream and rhubarb jam once they are cooled. Not until all the pancakes are ready do I realize we're making them for the second-year girls. I thought the plan had been to make them for the guys. I'm unsure whether the plan changed or if I had it wrong from the beginning.

The male students continue coming in to check on what we're doing and to steal a few pancakes. When we start making hot chocolate, I run upstairs for the bag of miniature marshmallows my parents sent me. The marshmallows are a big hit with everyone except Sigrún, who complains that they have no taste. We carry the trays of pancakes and hot chocolate to the library, light candles at each table, and then invite the second-year girls. For the rest of the meeting, the girls are concerned that the boys might be listening. Someone periodically opens the door to check, and we continue our meeting in whispers. We decide that this Saturday night at the school dance, all the Bifröst girls will wear a pendant to distinguish us from the visiting Varmaland girls. Just before the meeting ends, we sing, *Good night, Ladies*, in English as everyone takes a photo of one another simultaneously, resulting in a stream of light from the synchronized camera flashes. Then it's off to bed at one in the morning.

Success. This is the first morning I avoid hearing the loud wake-up pounding and manage to stay asleep until eight o'clock. When I tell Alla Rúna what time it is, she jumps out of bed, dives into her clothes, and flies out the door. I take my time since I decide to skip breakfast.

The group dynamics teacher tells us we will be given an impromptu test with seven minutes to complete. This causes great stress on my part. When I look at the first line, it says to read the entire test before beginning. So I try to, though I don't have an inkling of what each sentence means. I skip down to the last line. I'm almost positive the instructions say, *When you finish reading this carefully, only answer number one*, which is to print your name. I do just that. I look up at the teacher and smile. I see all the others racing away to answer each question. When the seven minutes are up, all the students groan when they realize the last line of instructions.

That evening as the dinner and dance are about to begin, the Varmaland girls enter through the main school entrance, all dressed up in shades of black and white, with high heels and lipstick. It feels like a scene right out of a movie with the guys eyeing the pretty girls arriving from the nearby school. We enter the lounge room, and each Varmaland girl is paired with a male student. To be funny, as they're introduced, the Bifröst guys bow and kiss the girls on their hands.

This evening's entertainment consists of various short skits. The overall theme seems to be the male students making fun of women, using racy references. I don't know the precise language. The visuals are bad enough. Then the political economics teacher and a second-year student play the theme song from *Deliverance* on guitar and banjo.

These skits are followed by a mock Miss World competition. I get a sick feeling in my stomach when I discover that Þór is wearing my pink polka-dotted nightgown that the girls borrowed from me. I wonder if he knows I'm the owner of that nightgown. A second-year student is playing Miss USA, dressed in a blue swimsuit with a long robe, making him look incredibly tall and skinny. I'm shocked when Þór, adorned in my old worn-out nightgown, wins the contest.

When the school band starts to play, I'm impressed with their talent. This evening, the Bifröst guys must dance the first half hour with the Varmaland girls they've been assigned to. Even when the time is up, the male students continue to dance with their assigned partners. That's fine with me. This way, I don't have to worry about why I don't have a male partner. I dance with two second-year girls, Lára and Beta, whom I've been getting to know better.

We do the Icelandic *gamal dans* (old dance), a mixer with all the girls in the outside ring and the guys in the center. When each round is finished, everyone ends up with a new partner. Now that I'm familiar with these dances, I'm having a lot of fun. At midnight, I help set out the ice cream on the tables for evening *kaffi*. Then the students whistle and cheer for the band to start again.

I look around at how everyone's dressed since the fashion here differs from Green Bay. The trend here is more conservative and a little dressier. The girls tend to wear their hair short and tightly curled, and for the dances, they wear solid-colored or lightly flowered dresses or jeans with turtleneck sweaters. Nothing too bright, tight, or low cut. For example, this evening, Guðrún, from my first-year class, is wearing a loose-fitting white dress with a shawl and white bobby socks with black leather Icelandic clogs like mine. While I've taken an interest in what everyone is wearing, I had no idea that anyone at Bifröst paid attention to what I wear. Recently, several girls have asked if I would loan them my red polyester flared pants. It's fun to look out on the dance floor to see Gugga wearing them.

At one-thirty, a man comes to say that the bus has arrived for the Varmaland girls and that this will be the last song. Everyone is thrilled when the band offers to play an extra half hour. I guess the bus driver will have to wait. I resolve to stay until the end since I don't want to return to the room knowing Alla Rúna is there with her friends. I stay until the band plays the last song.

I stop in the library in the morning and discover some books on the national parks of Iceland. I find a section describing Bifröst as "surrounded by grandiose, typically Icelandic landscapes of blue mountains and silvery rivers." The description sounds more picturesque than reality.

We have yet another Grábrók Club meeting this evening for both first- and second-year students. I'm unsure what this meeting is about until I learn that Kristján and Sigrún have been crowned this year's school king and queen. It's no secret that they are the most devoted-in-love couple in the school. Then I see all the students crowding around a poster on the wall near the cafeteria with everyone's names listed on the side. I discover this is a "love chart." Beside my name is a symbol lined up with Daði's name that means, "he will, but she won't," and next to Þór's name, "he will, and she will."

While being included makes me feel a little less like an outsider, I wonder how anyone could be aware of my private thoughts. If any guys in this school have caught my attention, it would be both Þór and Daði. Yet, I have never let on or said a word about them.

I'm impressed by all the hearts Kristján and Sigrún have received. Every romance is awarded points, with 100 points required for a red heart. Alla Rúna and Ásla tell me that Sigrún doesn't think it's an honor to be named school queen, while I think how embarrassing it is to have my secret fantasies broadcasted on a poster for all to see. It makes me wonder, did Þór or Daði provide this information?

I'm unsure how to react when I see Þór in the hall. He gives his customary salute like usual, so I imagine our friendship will go on as before, regardless of the poster. As for Daði, since he's a second-year student, I rarely see him other than our brief encounters, so I don't expect anything to change.

I gather my two cameras (one for slides and one for prints), boots, and jacket the following day and head out for *útivist*. As soon as I step out the door, I feel the cool freshness and joy from escaping the cooped-up loneliness inside the school doors. The initial sense of freedom from being out in the cool air doesn't last long. None of the other girls have chosen to walk today. Putting one foot in front of the other becomes an effort, especially on slippery ice. It usually takes me about twenty minutes to reach the Glanni Waterfall. Today it takes an hour.

When I reach the waterfall and see how clear and exquisite it looks, I'm convinced that the cold, windy walk is worth it. I read in my guidebook that the waterfall is on the river Norðurá and is believed to be home to elves and gnomes, something the Bifröst students like to talk about.

On this occasion, I do not encounter any elves or gnomes while at the falls. However, I get a big scare when I step into the snow, and my foot sinks about two feet deep. When I cautiously attempt another step, my other foot slips even deeper. I imagine the school staff sending out a search party and finding me here, frozen in the snow, several days later. Slowly, I work my way out of the deep snow and onto a sturdier surface. When I return inside, I try to forget my troubles by having a cup of tea for *kaffi*.

Kolla from my class explains that all the girls will dress up and sit together for dinner this evening. She warns me, Don't let any of the guys sit with us. I dress in a white, brown, and black print cotton dress, silver earrings, and a brown agate necklace and ring, with white barrettes in my hair. It still strikes me as funny how secretive and important the girls treat the Grábrók Club activities. Down in the cafeteria, all the girls are ready, sitting at a table with vases of flowers, a white tablecloth, and champagne glasses. All the guys are upset that the girls are doing this, so they push their tables further away and decorate their own tables with artificial plants. The girls stand up defiantly, so I do as well. We toast, *Skál* (Cheers!) with our water-filled champagne glasses.

A few days later, another Grábrók Club meeting is held in the library. We sing a few songs while the girls anticipate what the boys must be thinking, between giggles and chocolate crunch bars. We hear several guys banging on the door as we chant in Icelandic, Down with the boys! The loud banging continues. When we leave the library, all the guys are lined up in the hallway, saluting each of us as we pass by. When I return upstairs, I discover the boys' response to our meeting has been to remove our dorm room doors.

During evening *kaffi*, a girl approaches me about singing an American song for the school anniversary celebration, with Þór playing the accompaniment. I look at her in disbelief. What's this? Is she asking me to sing a solo? She must have assumed I have a good voice since I attend chorus practice. This isn't a reasonable assumption. I talk with Þór and the girl about how I actually don't have a good singing voice. They protest and say, Just listen to the song. I wait in the lounge. Eventually, Þór calls me in and plays the song on his harmonica. I have to laugh when he tells me, It's the blues. You don't need a good voice for this kind of song.

Þór stops in my dorm room the following day during a class break to give me the tape of the song to practice, reawakening my nerves. He tells me, You'll have to skip *útivist* today to copy down the lyrics so we can practice tonight. Why, when I'm finally being asked to participate, does it have to be something I have no talent for? I'm having trouble deciphering the lyrics with the noise in the hallway and no door to close. All the guys are asking, Are you missing something? Where's your door? Þór stops in to ask how the lyrics are coming along. As I listen to the song, I realize it just isn't meant for me. I know I wouldn't be able to sing it well.

My stomach is fluttering with butterflies over the thought of telling Þór I won't be performing the song. I bump into him on the way to chorus practice.

Þór tells me, Rehearsal tonight.

Nei, nei.

Já, já.

No, I mean that.

Really, for real?

Þór pats me on the shoulder and says, Alright. It pains me to see the disappointment in his eyes.

Another adventure that provides more outside time is the first-year students' trip to Reykjavík. Luckily, that includes me! I manage to plan for Jón to pick me up so I miss the exams. I visit briefly with Ásta in Borgarnes before taking the bus to Reykjavík to stay with Svandís and family. I'll spend the weekend with them before the first-year students arrive on Monday for the school trip around Reykjavík.

By coincidence, I've learned that Glen, the Rotary exchange student in Akureyri, will be in Reykjavík this weekend. Svandís asks Haukur if Glen can join us on the school trip. Haukur agrees. It's nice to have a chance to chat with another exchange student and share stories about learning Icelandic. Svandís is not pleased to have two Rotarian exchange students on her hands for the weekend, especially when Birgir, her husband, is in the Kiwanis Club. She is so frustrated with the Rotarians that she calls the President of the Iceland Rotary Club. I think this has made him feel guilty, so he and his wife come to pick Glen and me up. They take us around the outskirts of Reykjavík to see the hot water storage tanks and the hot springs.

Monday morning, Svandís drops Glen and me off downtown to start the tour with the Bifröst students. The first part of this adventure begins with a long, incomprehensible lecture as we tour an insurance company. During lunch, Glen complains about how boring it is listening to a talk he can't understand on Icelandic insurance. He sits beside me with a sickened look on his face when the afternoon lecture continues to be about insurance. His face lights up when Haukur announces that we will pay a visit to the President of Iceland later today.

Before meeting the President, we are invited inside the Alþing (the Icelandic parliament). I'm thrilled to have the opportunity to see the parliament in session, even when it's difficult to follow, with all the formalities in hushed voices. Afterward, we enter the courtyard of a small church. Without any pomp or circumstance, in walks Kristján Eldjárn, the President of Iceland.

We sit on the hard, wooden church pews, listening to the President welcome us. I'm thinking how unusual it is that the President can take two hours out of his busy day just to talk to us, without any staff or security around. When he's finished his speech, we are led to the lobby of his house.

Glen is desperate to get a photo of himself together with the President. Glen says to me, This is a chance of a lifetime. When we sign our names in the guest book, Glen insists, Tell Haukur you want to talk to the President, and then we'll get special attention. I try to ignore Glen by going to the adjoining room to take photos of Guðrún and Þórinn treating themselves to the hors d'oeuvres on the trays. When all the other students leave, except for Glen and me, I explain to the President that we are exchange students from the United States. It's a thrill to talk with him and his wife, even when I'm embarrassed that my Icelandic might not be comprehensible. At the end of our conversation, Glen and I take photos of each other with the President and his wife.

Now we've returned to Bifröst after the excitement of meeting the President. I leave the cafeteria to practice typing until the teacher interrupts me to say, You have a phone call. The call is from Johanna, the girl Ásta and Jón invited to their house in Borgarnes. It's not until now that I realize she is the receptionist's daughter.

She asks, Can you come over tonight? I want to show slides of my trip to New Zealand.

I'd like to, but I have chorus practice until nine.

Come whenever you can. You must ask Haukur to keep the doors open.

I explain to Alla Rúna about my visit to Johanna's tonight. She frowns and then grabs me by the sleeve to direct me to the bookkeeping teacher. I explain to him that I need the front door left open late. The teacher teases, You'll just have to sleep outside tonight. While escaping this place is difficult, getting back in is just as challenging.

———◇———

All these years later, my reflections about Bifröst did not bring as many rainbows followed by happiness as I would have hoped. Seeing the *Alþing* (Icelandic parliament) in session and the opportunity to meet Iceland's President provided a lot of excitement. Printing photos in the darkroom offered magical moments that later inspired me to become a freelance photographer. It was exhilarating to escape from the cramped quarters inside, to the fresh cool air outside during *útivist*. I could have better utilized those stuffy indoor hours at Bifröst. Rather than admonishing myself for not making sense of advanced bookkeeping, any students or teachers might have spared some time to tutor me in Icelandic. Had I known better, I would have spent more time taking photos outside and working in the darkroom.

What a relief that I didn't let anyone persuade me to perform that solo blues song. Luckily, I had enough sense to not make a total fool of myself. What is still astonishing to me is the irony of being sent to a boarding school as a high school exchange student. Without a host family, I lived in a dormitory with students much older than me who were smoking, drinking, watching pornography, and having sex.

CHAPTER 8

Hallo Akureyri!

"*Áfram með smjörið.*"
Literal meaning: On with the butter.
Intended meaning: Keep moving ahead.

The school trip to Akureyri is for second-year students. I've asked permission to go along since I believe a cultural trip will teach me more than sitting in a classroom with subjects I can't follow. I'm eager to get acquainted with Akureyri, Iceland's second-largest city, famous for its harbor and church. I don't know how I'll find the patience to get through two more weeks of school until we leave.

One bit of excitement is that I get to participate in two choir performances. Since I've been attending rehearsal twice a week, sometimes even without the director, we now have a set of ten Icelandic songs to perform. Following our afternoon classes, we take the bus to Borgarnes to give a concert at the nursing home. Of the repertoire, my favorite song is *Kenndu Mér Að Kyssa Rétt* (Teach Me To Kiss Right), although it's challenging to sing since the lyrics make me want to laugh. In addition to the Icelandic songs, we also sing *Amazing Grace*, which is especially fun since I don't have to worry about mispronouncing any of the words. Later in the week, we give another choir performance at Bifröst. Singing in a choir gives me an incredible feeling of togetherness and a sense of accomplishment, much more than singing a blues solo.

Another occurrence is the male retaliation against the girls' Grá-brók Club. Ever since the club was initiated, and even since the girls' doors were removed, I have suspected that the male students might dream up another way to retaliate. Early one morning, as I walk down the steps towards the lounge area, several boys start shouting my name, *Pála, Pála*! Followed by, *Pála* is in Grábrók!

Three guys, Þór, Ingi, and Guðmundur, pick me up by the arms and legs and start carrying me downstairs. *Nei, nei*, I scream out. I tickle all three in their armpits to try to make them put me down. The tickling distracts them but doesn't prevent them from carrying me to the showers and launching me under the bitterly cold water. I hear the other girls screaming at the shock of the water gushing over their hair and ears. The colder I get, the more I shout, *No*, no, no! In my fury, the English *No* sounds stronger than anything I can say in Icelandic.

Now I need to dry off and escape to peace and quiet outside. I smile when I smell the familiar chilly air—clear, crisp, and sunny. I take a different route than usual by walking to the curve in the road and down to the bridge, where all I can see is the long span of lava and green moss across the horizon.

When I return to my room, I have visitors. The English teacher, Guðmundur, and my former classmate, Pálmi, have come from Borgarnes to interview me for the school newspaper. While these are the only visitors I've ever had, Alla Rúna insists that we go somewhere other than "her room" to conduct the interview. We head down to the lounge area, where I discover that neither Guðmundur nor Pálmi have any questions prepared, and they have forgotten to bring a tape recorder.

Pálmi asks, What do you miss most from home?

Pizza. Then I add, Oh yes, and my family and friends.

This week, another bit of excitement is a long-distance call from my family in Wisconsin. While pretending to read an Icelandic newspaper in the lounge area, I'm called to the reception desk for a phone call from America. My heart races. This is the only call from my family since Christmas. All the students in the lounge area yell out to me, *Að bjóða heilsu* (Bid good health)!

I pick up the receiver and keep repeating, Hello? Hello? I hear the United States operator telling my mom to speak loudly, or she'll have to begin the call over again. My mom is too emotional to talk, so she hands the phone to my sister Dana. I have so much to say, but I'm worried I won't be able to fit it all in.

My sister tells me the family has decided not to visit me in March. She explains the plan. We will all come to Iceland in 1980 and then travel to Czechoslovakia (where my mom's parents originally came from).

When my mom comes back on, she's concerned about the idea of me traveling around Iceland without them but encourages me to do what I want. My dad gets on the line, Hello Smoky. It's endearing to hear his nickname for me based on the color of my eyes.

He says, We sent you a new camera flash attachment, chocolate Easter eggs and an extra writing journal. The package might not get there until August. I suppose you're doing lots of studying.

Not really.

I suppose you're doing just what they want you to be doing.

Dana takes the receiver again, and I ask, What are you eating for dinner? When she tells me pizza, I yearn for my family and home. I ask how much the Christmas phone call cost. She tells me it was 72 dollars. I say, You're kidding. We better hang up!

When we say goodbye, I have tears in my eyes. The students within hearing distance ask me if I would like to go home. I evade the question by telling them how much the last phone call cost.

My heart is rejoicing over the conversation with my family. It also leaves me with a wave of homesickness that's only partially off-set by Daði stopping by my room just to talk. I tell him how hard it was to speak English with my family. He says, You're beginning to think in Icelandic. When you go home, you'll think half in English and half in Icelandic, and it'll come out like German.

Today we depart for Akureyri. I learn that the bus ride will take eight hours. It's difficult to see much through the hazy window, except for a blurry view of mountains and snow. We stop at a coffee house along the way, where I buy a Coke because Daði raved about the taste the night before. Now that I'm paying closer attention, I think it is true, Icelandic Coke does taste exceptional. I've bought into the claim that the clear waters make it taste better in Iceland than elsewhere.

We stop in Blönduós, a small seaside town, where we pile into a cafeteria and are served a heavy meal of smoked mutton and potatoes for lunch. Also on our plates are the canned green peas (*grænar baunir*). I'm learning just how popular they are in Iceland and that they're often included with both lunch and dinner. As we drive on, the afternoon weather is getting sunnier and clearer. When we reach the hometown of my roommate's boyfriend, the bus stops to allow her to visit with him. We watch from the bus as they sit together in his car, hugging and kissing. After a few more kisses, she returns to the bus, and we are on our way. One of the students nicknamed Siggi leads a round of singing, giving me a feeling of togetherness. Then we stop at the small village of Varmhlíð to look around and eat ice cream at the coffee shop. Guðmundur points out a rack of postcards with Icelandic scenes, so I buy three and then photograph the snow-capped mountains surrounding us.

We reach Hotel Varnborg in Akureyri at seven in the evening. The teachers call out our hotel room numbers, and I'm relieved to be assigned a room with Lára. When Lára tells the woman behind the desk my name, the hotel receptionist turns to Lára to ask her in

Icelandic, Is she English? Again, I don't appreciate being referred to in the third person, as though I'm not there.

As we head out to get our first view of Akureyri, I hum an Icelandic tune, *Hallo Akureyri,* popular on the radio these days. I'm delighted to glimpse the city's most striking landmark, the Church of Akureyri, whose futuristic façade reminds me of something out of Batman's Gotham City with its geometrical twin towers. The architect was Guðjón Samúelsson, who also designed the central Hallgrímskirkja Church in Reykjavík. The Akureyri Church design was inspired by the rock formations of Iceland's Svartifoss waterfall.

Another breakthrough in my Icelandic happens during a house visit in Akureyri. Lára and I walk to the home of one of her mom's friends. Her warm and friendly welcome makes me feel like I've known her for years. When a student named Sigga stops in to visit, the biggest thrill for me is to realize that I can understand Lára's mom talking with me in the kitchen and still decern what Lára is saying to Sigga in the other room.

I'm amazed how Icelanders are so skilled at finding their way to the topic of dating, marriage, and kids in almost every conversation. Lára and her mom's friend tease me about how many kids I will have, predicting at least ten or twenty. I'm thinking, won't they be surprised, as I have a strong conviction to have none. We're served ice cream and coffee, and the host keeps exclaiming, These two flavors taste so good together! As if that wasn't enough to eat, she serves more coffee with cookies. I drink three cups of coffee during the visit, with my entire body jittery from the caffeine.

Before we leave, we're asked to sign the guest book. Our host pages through the book, showing me all her foreign visitors. Lára and I walk to our hotel and talk about dating and boyfriends until one in the morning. It sure feels good to have a friend to talk to as I hum myself to sleep.

A waker-upper knocks on our hotel room door in the morning, just like at Bifröst. When I discover breakfast isn't for another hour, it's a luxury to take a long shower before getting dressed. We eat breakfast at Hotel Kea, a few blocks away, then tour a paint and a plastic factory. The main conclusion I make is that I'd rather be outside than inside listening to presentations I can't discern.

We tour a newly built dairy, followed by a visit to the *Kaupfelag*, the primary department store in Akureyri. Afterward, we hike to Hotel Kea for lunch. My stomach feels bloated from the heavy meal, which is topped off with a sweet and robust cup of coffee. Just as we finish our coffee, we cross the street to tour a coffee roastery. Inside, the building has a strong, robust aroma of coffee. I think how my mom, a coffee connoisseur, would love it. After the tour, we are each served a large bowl of coffee soup. I don't know what is in this concoction. I must admit, I don't care for it.

The best part of the day is seeing the bright green grass covering the stairs up the hill to the Church of Akureyri. I take some photos to use when I give presentations to the Rotary Club upon my return to Wisconsin.

The afternoon lectures run on and on. It's funny to hear the same questions repeatedly asked, making me realize the students must have prepared the questions in advance. They always ask, How many people work here? What are the hours? At the end of each tour, when the question-and-answer period is completed, one of the students always stands up and gives a short speech to thank the tour guide. Siggi tells us that dinner is ready at Hotel Kea, and I'm thinking, just what I need to do, eat again.

Later that evening, I walk to the high school to visit Glen, my fellow American Rotary exchange student who joined me on the first-year student tour of Reykjavík. I feel lucky to have the chance to meet up again and exchange our experiences, even if we're struggling to speak Icelandic together. Glen admits that his Icelandic hasn't improved because he speaks "all too much" English with his friends.

In our room back at Hotel Varnborg, the older students are all talking together in drunken English. I'm offered a bottle of alcohol with "Martini" on the label. I take a sip and am surprised that the taste isn't all that bad. Then a few of the Bifröst guys ask if we'll walk outside with them. Lára immediately says no, speaking for both of us.

As it is getting late in the evening, I don't mind her speaking for me. Once the guys leave, Lára and I have an intense discussion about drinking and getting drunk. One of the male students comes knocking at our door. He jumps out of his boots, jacket, and sweater and tries to coax Lára into bed with him. Lára seems shocked and ends up leaving the room to avoid him. This is uncomfortable for me, as he stays in her bed for a while. Eventually, he leaves without disturbing me. I should let Lára know he's gone, but I have no idea where to find her.

I catch up on writing in my journal until Lára returns to our room. She tells me she was visiting the bus driver and another student upstairs. They told her if the male student hadn't left our room when she returned, they'd come help. She continues to inquire about the student to make sure he didn't make any passes at me. Her concern is a little late.

Even at this hour, Lára heads back upstairs to visit with some other students, staying several more hours. When she returns, I ask her if this has ever happened before, with guys coming into her room at night. She tells me, Not like this. She explains that she had two other invitations tonight but felt they were just making passes at her because they were drunk. She explains that they know she is a virgin and were making fun of her. She asks me if I've gone to bed with a guy, and I admit I have not.

In the morning, we're given an hour-long tour of a wool factory. I take lots of photos even in the dark lighting. Many sheep skins hang everywhere, which makes it interesting, except for the over-whelming putrid smell. Large, colorful spools of woven yarn are on display, including a striking shade of purple that makes me think of my mom since it's her absolute favorite color. We observe workers sewing jeans in an assembly line, cutting out the pockets, and then sewing the pieces together. Other workers are constructing the same shoes as the black Icelandic clogs all the female students wear (including me), cutting the leather pieces, stapling them together, painting the wood soles, and stamping labels on the bottom.

Once we've toured a wool factory, we tour another factory where they're assembling expensive leather coats and jackets. Next, we're driven to a ski hotel for a panoramic view of Akureyri. The weather is still frigid, so my fingers fumble as I try to release the camera shutter. Finally, we're dropped off at our hotel, and Glen arrives just as we enter the lobby. Lára and I were planning to go take photos, but Lára's tired, so I leave with Glen.

The second-year students from Bifröst look impressed as Glen and I walk past them. Their curious eyes are trying to figure out who this guy is. I feel foolish with all the hand motions Glen and I must use to follow one another's Icelandic. I take more photos of the harbor, the church, the swimming pool, and the high school. My body is aching from the cold wind and I go back to the hotel room to rest.

Glen returns after dinner so we can go to a movie called *Two Minute Warning*, starring Charlton Heston. It's loud and filled with violence. During the movie, I think how great it would be if I were attracted to Glen. It's clear that Glen is not the guy of my romantic dreams. When the movie is over, we stand outside talking in the cold. Glen thinks it's improper to come up to my room. I don't mind since I'm not worried he'll make a pass at me, so I invite him up, and we talk together in my room.

Glen warns me, You'll have a tough time in high school next year after living in Iceland. He thinks it'll be more of an adjustment going back than it was coming here. Maybe he thinks that way because he hasn't needed to make huge adjustments like I have. Once Glen leaves, I go down the hallway to the bathroom, past Sveinn and two others, Hörður and Elli, who don't say a word. They just give me long stares. On the way to my room, Hörður winks at me.

I had pictured tonight as a quiet evening to catch up on writing and sleep. Then I hear a knock on the door, and in come Hörður and Elli. I take their photos, and they write down their home addresses so I can visit them when I return to Iceland. Then Lára enters the room with a new guy who looks very handsome and is not from Bifröst.

I try to fall asleep. I can't because Lára and her new beau are in our room whispering to each other, their hands rustling all over one another. I learn that he's a seaman from Siglufjörður in the far north of Iceland. Now it's three in the morning, and I'm dead tired, but I can't sleep. Lára steps out of the room, and her new sweetheart explains to me in Icelandic, I'm just sleeping next to Lára, nothing else.

Lára returns, and they both undress while I continue to hear their whisperings and Lára's protests. I know the Icelandic as he asks her, Why won't you let me enter you? Then Lára explains, I have no pills. I don't want to. On and on, I hear their whispers. Eventually, I fall asleep, but not without a lot of anxiety.

Lára's new boyfriend is gone early in the morning, and we discuss the events of the night before. I'm not seeking an explanation, only she protests that she didn't have sex with him.

It's our last morning in Akureyri, so we pack up our luggage and then walk over to meet with the other students for a breakfast of smoked mutton on bread. Then we take the bus to the other side of Akureyri. As we pass by snow-capped mountains and glaciers, I would love to take a photo, but I can't ask the bus driver to stop.

Now we are visiting yet another dairy farm. Even before we get off the bus, my nose picks up a deep, unpleasant smell. We're told that the odor isn't due to the cows. Instead, it's a cleaning potion that is a combination of alcohol and ammonia. I've visited several Wisconsin farms and never seen such friendly cows as this. They lick the students' hands and bark like dogs as though they're crying for affection.

The last stop on our tour of Akureyri is a large and smelly chicken farm. Once inside the first farmyard building, we see countless tiny chicks. Their cuteness is in stark contrast to the gruesome sight in the next building where the farmworkers are killing the grown chickens. The smell inside is even more unbearable than outside. In the connecting room, the chickens are cut up and boxed to be sold and eaten. I don't think I'll ever be able to eat chicken again after witnessing the grotesque process. I'm surprised when several students and teachers buy boxed chickens to take home.

With our school tour completed, the bus driver drops us off at the Hotel Kea cafeteria, where, unlike the previous meals, we're told we're on our own to pay for lunch. Since it's expensive, many of us skip the hotel lunch. I cross the street with the others to buy the long, skinny *pylsur*. It's tricky to eat the hot dog while standing, with the sauce spilling out. Then Lára's new sweetheart comes driving past. He waves from the car window, motioning for Lára to come over so he can say goodbye.

The bus isn't available for our return trip, so we must fly back to Reykjavík. Lára informs me that her new boyfriend is giving her a ride to the airport. I ask if I can get a ride as well. When she returns, she starts out saying goodbye to me, making me think I won't be getting a ride. Then she laughs and tells me, I'm only kidding. It's uncomfortable in the car with Lára and her boyfriend making out in the backseat while the friend who's driving adjusts the mirror to get a better view of them. This new boyfriend sure makes Lára look beautiful. Ever since she's met him, she has had a permanent smile planted on her face.

Lára says her goodbyes to her boyfriend, and now we sit together with Óli and Snorri inside the tiny Akureyri airport. Óli has a bottle of alcohol in his hand. From the looks of it, he's already had a few too many. I'm happy to get a front seat on the plane, next to the window with a view. The take-off gives me a fright with a rocky start and a lot of turbulence. I'm pleased to get a perfect view of the colorful rooftops as we leave Akureyri. Once we're above the clouds, it's smooth sailing. We are flying over glaciers and geysers, but all I can see are the tops of puffy white clouds.

Getting permission to go along on the Akureyri trip with the second-year students was a smart move. While my primary interest was in the cultural aspects of Akureyri, it was an excellent way to escape being cooped up inside the tight quarters at Bifröst. The trip also expanded my knowledge of the agricultural and industrial aspects of Iceland. I interacted with the older students and had conversations with Lára on a more intimate level. It was eye-opening to witness the blossoming romance with her new boyfriend. At the same time, my interactions with Glen gave me insight into who I was, and was not, attracted to.

The words the Rotarian "Grandfather" Harwood wrote in his letter to my parents were starting to come to fruition. He predicted that my Iceland experience would foster growth from adolescence to adulthood. Socializing with the older students at Bifröst and on the Akureyri trip did indeed serve to speed up my coming of age.

Welcome to Borgarnes, the sign I took as a personal welcome.

The house in Borgarnes where I lived with Ásta and Jón.

Potato harvest with my host mother, Ásta and grandkids.

View of Borgarnes, with a population of 1,400 in 1977.

Paula with host parents, Jón and Ásta.

The sheep slaughterhouse in Borgarnes.

Christmas with my host family in Borgarnes.

View of central Reykjavík from Hallgrímskirkja Church.

One of the geothermal heated hot pools, next to an
outdoor swimming pool in Reykjavík.

The whale station in Hvalfjörður.

Bifröst Junior College, the boarding school I attended for four months.

Taking a walk for *útivist* (outside time) at Bifröst.

Frozen Glanni Falls, the waterfall that I frequented
from the Bifröst boarding school.

Paula with the President of Iceland (1968-1980),
Kristján Eldjárn, and his wife Halldóra Eldjárn.

Paula at Gullfoss Waterfall in 1978.

Paula at Gullfoss Waterfall in 2021.

Steaming lava on Heimaey, Vestmannaeyjar (Westman Islands).

Paula onboard the Esja cargo ship, ready to begin the
circle route around the circumference of Iceland.

The Esja cargo ship, unloading goods at one
of the stops on the circle route.

Isafjörður, one of the ports on the circle route.

View from onboard the cargo ship, Esja.

Sign that greeted Paula when she returned home. The sign was painted by high school friends and covered the entire front of the house. The photo appeared in the Green Bay Press-Gazette.

SPRING/VOR 1978

———◇———

CHAPTER 9

Coming Out of The Dark

"Að leggja höfuðið í bleyti."
Literal meaning: Lay your head in water.
Intended meaning: Take some time to figure things out.

As April approaches, the darkness is lifting a little each day. The brighter, lighter days are helping to improve my sense of well-being. The warmer weather means more time outside and taking off the heavier winter layers. With the weather improving, school ending soon, and more travel opportunities, my spirits are lifting.

Easter vacation is just around the corner, and I'm looking forward to visiting the Westman Islands, the largest island group off the south coast of Iceland. The invitation to visit Birgir's Aunt Anna, Uncle Addi, and their daughter Elisabet on Heimaey (Home Island), fulfills my desire to see more of Iceland. The visit will allow me to meet another family and learn more about Icelandic geography, history, and Easter traditions. I travel with Ásta Margrét and Vigfus on a small 25-seat plane. I'm happy when the flight attendant hands me an Icelandic newspaper, assuming I'm Icelandic. As we land, I enjoy the view of the harbor.

Icelanders commonly refer to the single island of Heimaey as "Vestmannaeyjar." The name includes an archipelago of 15 islands and 30 rock stacks formed by underwater volcanic eruptions. My first impression of the island is its overwhelming, permeating fish smell. On this small island, there is no escaping the strong odor.

The first day on the island, we re-discover a letter in a bottle. Birgir's Uncle Addi had found the note last winter while at sea. Ásta Margrét and I are excited to find it tucked away on a bookshelf. The letter is from Francisco Sandoval, who states that he is 27 years old, from Mexico, and asks anyone who finds the letter to write to him. The letter isn't dated, so we don't know how old Francisco is now. Since Addi hasn't gotten around to it, I plan to write to Francisco. (A few months later, I went to Mexico with my parents. We visited the town Francisco was from but couldn't track him down).

I have always wanted to see a still-steaming volcano, and visiting the island fulfills that dream. We hike up the mountainside of lava, where we can see a 5,000-year-old volcano. The one beside it erupted in 1973. Aunt Anna tells me about the tradition of baking bread in hot lava. Even after five years, the surface lava from this volcano is still hot enough to bake bread. I'm excited to get a glimpse of Surtsey from up on the volcano. Surtsey is a new island that emerged from the sea in 1963 during an eruption that lasted until 1967.

For dinner this evening, I eat puffin for the first time. This feels a bit strange, but the flavor is good and reminds me of ptarmigan or grouse.

Now that it's Easter Sunday, I have the opportunity to celebrate another holiday in Iceland. Svandís and Birgir fly in with Birgir Jón and Linda Björg, to celebrate Easter with Birgir's aunt and uncle. The highlight of Easter for the kids is to receive large chocolate eggs filled with candy. Birgir is disappointed since the ones he ordered from Germany haven't arrived yet, so the kids must wait until we return to the mainland for their Easter candy.

We sit down to an Easter meal of roasted lamb with glazed potatoes, red cabbage, green peas, and sweet pickles. As the family is not religious, we don't attend church services. Despite improving weather on the mainland, the skies at Vestmannaeyjar have turned stormy. Icelanders even have a special word for severe weather during Easter called *Paskahret.* While waiting for the weather to clear, we chat, gossip, and eat. Birgir shows me a book about the 1973 volcanic eruption that destroyed nearly one-third of the homes and buildings on the island. I'm impressed that Birgir is familiar with every photo in the book, including the names of the people and the owners of the houses. Already with four children, he has welcomed me into the family and shared many stories, celebrations, and activities.

The severe Easter weather has delayed our flight by a day. Now we're back on the mainland. I'm talking with Svandís in the kitchen. She is a nurse by profession, taking her job so seriously that she carries it through every aspect of her life. I admire what a good listener she is and her ability to get along so easily with everyone. I love how her eyelids flutter when she explains something she enjoys. After the visit to Vestmannaeyjar, I feel even closer to Birgir and Svandís, and I'm sad to leave for Bifröst since I'll miss their support.

Ásta and Jón have just returned to Svandís' apartment from their trip to the Canary Islands, and I'm eager to hear about their vacation. Ásta is relieved to be back in Iceland because she found it too hot, and she missed her favorite Icelandic foods. As I'm chatting with Ásta and Jón in the car on the way back to Borgarnes, a discussion of my hospital stay last November comes up. This is the first I've heard that I rode in an ambulance from Borgarnes to the Akranes Hospital. I'm trying to picture being lifted into the ambulance and then into the hospital on a stretcher. The added information is a shock since I have no memory of this, and no one has told me about it.

I talk with Lára about whether I'm learning enough here at Bifröst. Verbalizing the question makes me realize that I am—not only about Icelandic but in making new friends and fitting in better. I've also discovered how much I love photography from working in the darkroom. I know more about myself, where I'm at, and where I want to be. I think to myself, not bad for accomplishing this on my own at sixteen, in a foreign country, and here at this boarding school, without a host family.

With spring beginning and school ending soon, I am now finding opportunities to participate in class and fit in with my classmates. Guðmundur, the political economics teacher, explains a presentation the students will have to give. He assigns each student a topic to cover regarding various social issues, asking them to explain whether or not they are in support of the issue. He finishes assigning the topics and then Magnea and Sigrún complain that he forgot to include *Pála* (referring to me).

The teacher says he will call on me the next time, and I wonder when that will be. Following the break, the students continue to take the teacher to task for not involving me. As the teacher repeats the topics each student must discuss, my well-meaning classmates ask, What about Pála? Guðmundur asks me if he should skip me. The girls behind me protest.

The teacher returns to my desk with a sheet of paper and asks me in Icelandic, Are you for or against *laxveiði*?

What's *laxveiði*?

Something to do with fish.

With my heart pounding rapidly, I tell him, I think I'm for it.

Why? He asks and then tells me to write it down.

I ask Sigrún what she thinks. She shrugs her shoulders, laughs, and says, I'm for it.

Why?

Because it's fun, it's just a sport.

I write out a sentence until Guðmundur says, Time's up. I manage to squeeze out one more sentence.

The teacher calls out my name, *Pála*, and I head up to the front of the class. I attempt to say in Icelandic, I am for salmon fishing because it's fun to do and a nice activity during vacation. But it's not good to do too much of it because then there wouldn't be enough salmon.

I hear Sigrún behind me saying, That was excellent on your part. We're given a five-minute break, and then we return to class for the teacher to discuss our speeches. Guðmundur says, I know how difficult this is for the *útlandingur* (the foreigner), so I picked the salmon topic since I knew I'd covered it in class. He gives me a good grade for my short speech.

Now that I've just made a breakthrough in class participation, I'm also improving my personal conversations. For *útivist* today, I head outdoors with Lára, Beta, and Didda to take the long route all the way down past the river and Grábrók Crater. The girls start talking about their favorite food and beverages. I tell them about root beer since I know they don't have it here in Iceland, and they are curious about the flavor. I describe how delicious it tastes. They tell me about some of their favorite places in Iceland and then I explain what I think are the best places to visit in the United States.

Even as things lighten up, I'm grappling with the upsetting news about my oldest sister. The letter I received today from my mom has left me a little flabbergasted since she wrote that my sister has left her husband and is dating a guy she met dancing. I'm finding it difficult to accept this news without any previous knowledge of any marriage difficulties and without any family to help deal with the news.

Alla Rúna leaves to go to a play somewhere. I can't even think about going as I wrestle with the news about my sister. Instead of writing a letter directly to her, I write one to my parents, which ends up being six pages long. I feel a sense of accomplishment from writing it.

I go down to Lára's room since she told me she wasn't going to the play. I'm unsure whether to tell her the news about my sister, but

I need to discuss it with someone. She is sympathetic, only not when we get on the topic of children, and I tell her that I'm not planning to have any.

She tells me, It's much more shocking that you're not going to have any kids than that your sister is separating from her husband. I'm sure everyone in your family is highly intelligent, which makes it unfortunate that you're not going to have kids while others who aren't as smart will. I think it would be all right for you to have just one child.

This is her conclusion, even when I repeatedly explained my motivation is to help kids already here on this earth.

When I see Ásla's open door, I notice she's in her room alone, reading the newspaper. I stop to talk and end up discussing my summer plans with her, plans that change every time someone asks me about them. She gives me her phone number in case I travel south near her house in Skaftafell. I head downstairs to the shower room with Beta, Lára, and Didda, where I discover the hot water is all used up. This makes it impossible to keep my head under the freezing water long enough to finish rinsing my hair.

The girls are full of giggles. Their laughter and joyfulness help show me the brighter side of life since I'm still dealing with the grim news about my sister. They notice the tiniest details and then comment on them. Lára says to me, You still have shampoo in your hair. This is not news to me since I ran out of hot water. Meanwhile, Didda points out all the snarls in my hair, while Lára notices that my sweater is full of hair, and Beta chides me for using a backpack to carry my towel and cosmetics to the shower. Their teasing comments show me they have allowed me into their world. I have broken through the ice for a few precious moments and caught a rainbow.

Another adventure is to head off to a religious confirmation in Reykjavík via Borgarnes. Along the drive to Reykjavík, Ásta exclaims, Iceland can be so beautiful! I look out the car window and agree, as the country does take on a new, exciting look now that the ice and snow are gone and the green grass is sweeping across the landscape. I'm developing a deep attachment to the sight of Icelandic horses and sheep dotting the green countryside. We reach Svandís and Birgir's apartment in a record time of two hours and five minutes. A delicious meal of Icelandic cod is waiting for us. Svandís has a cute new haircut and is full of news about her upcoming work trip to Mallorca.

Ásta's not interested in attending the church confirmation ceremony, which is fine with me since I can imagine how dull it could be. I write in my journal until I need to dress for the reception.

I'm not entirely sure whose confirmation reception we are attending until we pull up to Gylfi's house, and I realize it's for Gylfi's younger brother, Helgi. Discovering that I know most of the guests at the reception makes me feel more at home since I can participate in the conversations. I'm introduced to a most unusual woman. She was born in Germany, lived in the United States for ten years, and in Iceland for several years. She speaks her own language, a mix of German, English, and Icelandic.

On the drive back to Borgarnes, Ásta explains, Quite a few people living in Iceland speak a strange combination of languages. They have no native language. Somehow, they survive since most Icelanders are multilingual.

Hearing that others have lived here longer than me and still aren't fluent in Icelandic makes me more confident about how much of the language I've mastered so far.

Back in my bedroom in Borgarnes, I stay in bed dreaming about returning to Wisconsin. I see long talks with my parents, sisters, and friends and the ability to chat freely and laugh when something is funny. Ásta comes into my room and shows me a photo of her, Jón, and me in Seltjarnarnes taken just before the wedding we went to last fall. I ask her, Where did this come from? Ásta says, Your parents sent it to us.

I've been sending my exposed film back to my parents, and once they had it developed, they must have picked out this photo to enlarge. My heart fills with warmth and appreciation that my parents were so thoughtful to send this. Ásta finds a frame for the photo and hangs it in the hallway beside all the other family portraits. Now I am officially a part of the family.

Jón asks me when I want him to drive me to Bifröst. This will be my last week at Bifrost, but still, I'd prefer to tell him never again. Ásta shows me how large the avocado seed has grown since we placed it in water at Christmas.

The weather on the way to Bifröst is sunny and clear until the fog sets in when we arrive. During my last few days at Bifröst, I'm determined to develop a more positive relationship with my room-mate, Alla Rúna. I get out my recipe book, a topic I've found she's interested in, and we spend a half hour going over recipes. Seeing that she is in better spirits, I tell her, You must feel good that your exams will be done soon, and then you get to travel to Mallorca. I should have known she couldn't stay positive for long. She says, I'd rather just forget about going. I'd prefer to stay home, relax, and drink *brennivín* (a strong Icelandic liquor).

Alla Rúna has started reading *Kidnapped*, a book I loaned her, and since she enjoyed it, this gives us another positive point of discussion. I'm going to lend her the book I just finished reading, *The Picture of Dorian Gray* by Oscar Wilde, which is full of paradoxes. I copy an interesting paragraph:

> *It is better not to be different from one's fellows. The ugly and the stupid have the best of it in this world. They can sit at their ease and gape at the play. If they know nothing of victory, they are at least spared the knowledge of defeat. They live as all should live – undisturbed, indifferent, and without disquiet.*

While I've made small gains to establish a more positive connection with Alla Rúna, this passage makes me think about how not one person in this world is perfectly content. While it's impossible to make everyone else happy, I can try to be content with who I am and where I am.

Back in our dorm room following dinner, still aiming for positivity, I present Alla Rúna with a going-away gift of a silver bracelet. I picked the right gift for her since she gives me a kiss, quite an unlikely reaction coming from her, and I feel content that I've finally won her over.

Alla Rúna's boyfriend has come to spend the night. Tomorrow is everyone's last day at Bifröst. She asks me if I can manage to sleep in another room tonight since her boyfriend will be staying over. I check with Þórey if I can stay with her, and when she agrees, I transport my bedsheets and quilt downstairs to her room.

Meanwhile, I see Guðrún in the hallway, and she suggests that we go visiting. We head to Beta and Didda's room. The girls talk about their ratings for *útivist* and how unfair it is to be graded on the number of times they went outside. Then we all share our summer travel plans. We say goodnight, and I head to Þórey's room. She's not there. I'm so tired that I climb into the top bunk and say good night to myself for one last time at Bifröst.

Þórey is waking me to tell me I was having a bad dream. My eyes focus, confirming a male stranger is in the room. Þórey seems to know him, and I hear her talking with him in the lower bunk. It sounds as if he's in bed with her, and they are discussing how strange it is that I awoke so startled. They laugh about the scared look on my face.

The male stranger tells Þórey that he could tell from the look on my face that I wasn't Icelandic, and then he asks her where I'm from. I hear Þórey telling the guy that she's tired and not to bother her, and then he asks her something about coming up to me. It's the middle of the night, and I'm still half asleep. I can't think or say anything as this strange man, several years older than me, takes off his coat and climbs the wooden ladder up to my bunk.

The stranger could be a Bifröst alumni student. I have no idea of his name or anything about him other than at this moment, he has climbed into the top bunk with me. He starts asking me questions, and I answer in a scared whisper, holding tight onto my quilt until he pulls it out from under my hold so he can slide under it. He forces his tongue inside my mouth and tries to push his finger inside me. I use all my strength to move his hand away. How unbearable, this man getting pleasure off me. It makes me feel numb, without a voice. I feel embarrassed and ashamed and find what is happening to me incomprehensible. Then he rubs his hand over my buttocks, and I squeeze them together tight, so he can't move his hand in between. He keeps sticking his tongue inside my mouth, causing me to feel nauseous.

All I want is to get him out of here. I hear Þórey wake up and leave the room. Finally, when I think the stranger is sound asleep, I use all my energy to push him aside so I can climb over him and down the wooden ladder out of the bunk bed to safety.

What a relief to be out of the crowded bunk bed and able to do something as simple as combing my hair until the stranger wakes up and asks for water. I use the sink in the room and give him some. When he climbs down the ladder, he repeatedly tells me he's sorry. He says in English, American girls are so pretty, so completely different from Icelandic girls.

I'm thinking, what a bunch of baloney. The stranger offers to give me a ride to Borgarnes. All I want is for him to leave. He kisses me, puts his hand around me, and then good riddance, I'm alone and safe.

Now that it is morning, Þórey comes back in and tells me, You're welcome to stay in bed for as long as you want. That's the last thing I want to do. I can't return to my dorm room as Alla Rúna is still there with her boyfriend. I desperately need fresh air, so I head to

Glanni Falls for one last round of photos. Then one last shower at Bifröst. With Þórey and Sigrún, we walk up the hill to the store to buy Cokes. Finally, the coast is clear for me to return to my room. I drag my quilt and pillow back upstairs and finish packing.

Out in the front school yard, I photograph the first-year students in one large group, followed by the second-year students, as everyone prepares to leave. The reality of this moment turns out to be completely different from what I envisioned. Instead of all the students saying goodbye to me as I drive away, I'm the last student left since Ásta and Jón don't arrive until later in the afternoon. When Olga, the receptionist, insists that they stay for *kaffi*, I'm disappointed. All I want to do is to leave. Finally, goodbye, Bifröst.

I would have liked to end this chapter with a triumphant "coming out of the dark" moment instead of a traumatic event. Despite the continued dark experiences, these months still represented a gradual progression out of the dark for me.

I'm not sure precisely what Ásta and Jón originally signed up for. Technically, they could have just wished me well and forgotten about me for the remaining part of my stay. Instead, after I was sent to boarding school, they continued to play the role of a host family, taking care of me over the holidays and inviting me for weekends. I kept imagining that they would come to rescue me from Bifröst and say, Come back to us in Borgarnes. I knew this wasn't a realistic possibility. I couldn't allow myself to give up and persevered to make it through these difficult months.

With great reluctance, I included the stranger in my bed incident as it remains very troublesome for me. I couldn't write the words without shaking and feeling terribly angry and confused. What hurts most is that I was too naïve to speak up or to recognize how invasive the incident was. Given the magnitude of what happened to me that last night at Bifröst, I struggled to learn from this horrible event, so I could move on and come out of this without huge scars.

When I look back and count the number of times I was kissed, touched, or addressed inappropriately by older men as a teenager of sixteen, I ask myself, was it a product of the times? Was it a product of the circumstances? I was sent to dances and events where the participants were generally much older than me. Were sexual advances and liberties taken because of differences in age? These questions remain unanswered, yet these instances have made me more aware of others who get stuck in similar situations. This makes me want to do anything possible to help them.

On the other hand, I met many different people from various settings during my year of study in Iceland. As a teenager, it would be expected for romantic interests to form. When I look back, the flirtations I engaged in were fleeting, innocent, and insignificant. In fact, during my entire stay, I never went on an actual date. These flirtations would probably have been forgotten if I hadn't kept a journal.

That I survived four months at the boarding school was indeed a coming out of the dark moment. Not only did the weather get warmer and the days brighter, but I also climbed through all the hurdles, did my best to make friends, and became adept with the language and culture.

I was eager to share knowledge of my home country with Icelanders and bring home knowledge about Iceland's geography, customs, and culture. I wanted to travel the country to become familiar with the fjords, the mountains, the rivers, the waterfalls, and the glaciers. That's my objective in the following chapters.

CHAPTER 10

Exploring Iceland

"Rúsínan í pylsuendanum."
Literal meaning: The raisin in the end of a hot dog.
Intended meaning: Discovering a good surprise, or the icing on
the cake.

School's out. Time to travel! I want to explore as much of Iceland as possible. My plan is to travel first to Reykjavík and then embark on an Icelandic Touring Club excursion to Þórsmörk. I'll be roughing it in a valley in the South Highlands of the country between the mountain glaciers of Tinkfjallajökull and Eyafjallajökull. Þórsmörk is known as a watery wonderland with endless hiking trails.

Anna gives me a ride to Reykjavík. We're having dinner at her parents' house in the nearby town of Kópavogar, until it's time to board the tour bus. Anna warns me, With the rainy weather, the roads to Þórsmörk will be wet and slippery. The bus will likely get stuck, so you may have to walk part of the way. I'm not sure whether to take her warning seriously. While I'm gaining experience packing for weekend excursions, I've still ended up without a raincoat or winter underwear for this out-of-the-way destination.

Anna stops at her brother's house to pick up a raincoat for me to use. Then she takes me to the neighborhood grocery store where I'm to purchase provisions for my trip. While I wander through the aisles, Anna looks at me, dismayed. She can tell I'm clueless about what to purchase. I don't want to appear incapable under her watch-ful eyes, so I try to remember what my parents would bring on our family camping trips. Iceland's groceries aren't the same as back in Wisconsin, making it more complicated to determine what I might need. I sheepishly select a package of Icelandic hot dogs and buns, rye bread, butter, milk, tea, a few fruits and vegetables, and my es-sential pack of chewing gum. The groceries would have cost half as much back in Wisconsin.

The rain is pounding on the hood of the car when Anna drops me off at the tour bus. She tells me, It's good practice for your future trips, going to Þórsmörk in this weather. I know it would be wiser to travel in the summer months when the weather is better, only school's out now, and I'm dying to see more of the country. This is the most exciting trip I could find offered this time of year.

Happy excursion, I tell myself as the bus heads on its way with eight other tourists, the tour guide, and the driver. The guide is in her 40s, very outdoorsy in her khaki pants and jacket. Since I've been speaking only Icelandic for months, I can barely follow her when she speaks to me in English. Two teenage girls in the back of the bus give me an unwelcoming glare as I force a friendly smile back. I start up a conversation with the woman across the aisle from me. She has grey hair, looks like she's in her early 60s, and traveling alone. We converse for a while in Icelandic and I'm rewarded when she says she didn't realize I was a foreigner until I told her.

Now I see what Anna was referring to. With the heavy rain, the bus must cross several rivers and streams that have flooded the road. The water rushes up against the sides of the bus. I feel much safer inside the bus than getting out to walk, as Anna had teasingly sug-gested. At exactly midnight, we reach the small, wooden Þórsmörk shelter. When I step off the bus, I can barely see even a few feet in front of me, with nothing but fog beyond that. We unload our baggage and enter the shelter to discover the caretaker has a fire snapping in the old cast iron stove.

The grey-haired lady from the bus shares some hot coffee with me. It soothes my throat, which started to ache during the bus ride. I'm unsure where I'm supposed to sleep until the tour leader directs me around a narrow corner to a small, bare room devoid of furniture except for a few bunk beds and cots.

I light the single candle in the room and then tear off and chew on a chunk of Icelandic rye bread until I need to go to the bathroom like something terrible. It must be outside, so I open the shelter door and head out. I can't see a thing through the fog. I'm lucky no one can see me peeing behind the shelter.

Back inside, I dress in the warmest clothes I brought: my tights, wool socks, Levi cords, a blouse, a cardigan, and my Icelandic wool sweater. I snuggle into my sleeping bag on the wooden cot and pull a wool blanket over the top. Once I say goodnight to the two teenage girls sharing the room, I blow out the candle.

It was a rough night, constantly twisting and turning to get warm. The cot was so uncomfortable that I kept getting terrible cramps in my calves, unable to move without intense pain. From all the tossing, my hair is in snarls, covering my eyes and mouth. Using the old kettle on the wood stove, I make a cup of tea to soothe my throat. Then I cut two slices of rye bread, top them with butter and cucumber slices, and drink more hot tea. I'm amazed at how hungry I am, even without having done any hiking. Our tour guide informs us, With so much wind and rain outside, it doesn't make sense to go out.

I start up a conversation with the two girls and learn they're both fifteen years old. The other guests are washing and scrubbing the rooms as I page through the guest book and read the raving reviews written by previous visitors. Obviously, they were smarter to visit when the weather allowed them to hike the trails and view the glaciers. There's nothing left to do in this fog and misty rain but prepare lunch. For me, that's two hot dogs, plus milk and tea. The hot dogs are disappointing since I have to eat them cold. Apart from the kettle that was provided, I didn't know we needed to supply our own cookware. The unappetizing hot dogs are difficult to swallow while smelling the savory grilled hamburgers the two girls are eating.

After several card games with the girls, the rain eases up a bit. I attempt to venture outside. I can't believe my eyes when I gaze through the heavy fog at the glistening, overflowing rivers, streams, brooks, and waterfalls in every direction. Numerous hiking paths and bridges decorate the landscape, with splotches of green grass in between. I'm soaking wet from the rain but inspired by the magnificent flowing water views. I definitely need to come back here when the weather is better.

The rain has soaked through my pants, underwear, and shoes. I change into dry pants and the dry wool socks that Ásta knitted for me. The tour guide tells us, We can't hike the trails given the fog and heavy rain. Since the weather won't be getting any better, we'll be packing up and leaving.

I'm disappointed I've come all this way just to sleep, eat, and play cards. At least I obtained one brief, exhilarating glimpse of Þórsmörk's grandeur.

Our bus leaves at five in the afternoon, re-crossing the rivers and streams. The shelter caretaker is smoking a pipe directly behind me on the bus. The pipe smoke circling around my head adds to the ache in my throat, making me feel I might pass out. Then I see a bright, full rainbow as we pass directly alongside the expansive Eyafjallajökull glacier. While this trip has brought nothing but rain, fog, and smoke until now, at least I have a bright, colorful rainbow to add to the experience.

I catch a partial view of the glacier framed by the rainbow until thick clouds set in, making it difficult to observe any more of the countryside. We stop at a Nesti gas station for a snack. I'm tempted by the strong aroma of the French fries, briefly interested in a type of soda called malt, and settle on an ice cream sundae. When the sundae is delivered to me, I don't see any chocolate sauce until I discover it hidden under the ice cream.

We reach Reykjavík three and a half hours later. I head inside the bus station to call Anna, who is expecting me to stay with her at her parent's house. I can't get through to her with the number I have. No luck calling Svandís either. I can't look up Anna's parents' number since I don't know her father's second name. I'm rescued by the lady from the bus, who searches through all the Ólafs in the phone book. When she finds the one on Græntunga (Green Tongue), I recognize the street name, and finally, I get through.

Sunday, Anna takes her kids and me to the largest swimming pool in Reykjavík. I enjoy swimming the long length of the Olympic-size pool and then popping in and out of each of the four small, circular, hot pools. As soon as I enter the hottest one, my body goes numb. This is a good numbness since it removes the leftover anxiety from the Þórsmörk misadventure and puts me in a state of total relaxation.

After my swim, Anna drops me off downtown. I'm delighted to be alone, content to rely on my creative resources. I window shop and then enter a small café to order a chocolate milkshake, my first in Iceland, but not without feeling guilty since my diet has gone astray. During my stay, I'm constantly reminded of the warning about how exchange students gain weight. With Ásta's heavy cooking and the big servings at Bifröst, it's been a constant battle to avoid rich and starchy foods. I walk alongside the reflecting pool and watch the dabbling ducks. I feed my passion for photography as I snap photos of the national theater and library and then walk around Ingólfur Square to the number three bus stop. When I climb onto the bus, it's a delight to find Svandís' sons, Birgir Jón and Vigfus, on board.

The next big event is to celebrate my birthday in Iceland. When Ásta arrives at Svandís' apartment, she hands me letters from my mom and dad and my sister Dana, a birthday card from my friend Laura and a letter from my sixth-grade teacher, Mr. Hoffman. Dad writes a lengthy discussion on how to argue that there's overpopulation. Mom is all worked up because her "baby girl" is turning 17.

In the morning, I wake up from a deep sleep, suddenly conscious that today is my seventeenth birthday. Ásta enters the TV room where I've been sleeping, carrying a beautifully wrapped birthday gift under her arm. I tear open the wrapping paper to discover a lovely hand-crafted silver bracelet. Ásta says, It's made by an Icelander, only found here. I open the gift Anna gave me yesterday, a necklace with a stunning white Icelandic stone and a pair of matching earrings.

Svandís asks me how we celebrate birthdays back home. I get sentimental about all the special birthday parties my parents have organized for me. Svandís and Ásta leave to pick up my birthday cake. I take Linda Björg out to the playground and see the mothers dropping off their kids, with one woman overseeing the play area. I enjoy pushing Linda Björg and some other children on their swings.

When I return to the apartment with Linda Björg, we have *kaffi*, including the cream cake Ásta and Svandís bought for my birthday. It's topped with cherries, pineapple, whipped cream, and seventeen birthday candles. Once I blow all the candles out, I learn that everyone is leaving for either a meeting or an appointment tonight, and I will be left home alone. Ásta doesn't remember that she offered to take me to dinner on my birthday. I'm sad I have nothing to do except sit alone in the lounge room and watch a TV re-run.

I've been sick with the stomach flu for several days since my birthday. I spend the time resting and writing in my journal. Now that I'm feeling better, I'm ready to plan another tour. I've booked a day trip to Hveragerði, Gullfoss Waterfall, and Þingvellir National Park. Since no one can give me a ride to the tour bus, I must take a taxi. I want to show that I can travel alone. Once in the cab, I realize I don't have enough money for the fare. I call Svandís, who speaks with the taxi driver. He agrees to allow me to pay the remaining amount upon my return.

So much English is spoken on this tour since it's for foreigners. An elderly man asks me questions in English and I can follow him fine, although responding in English is awkward. How strange and tired my mouth feels from speaking English. Icelandic words keep slipping in, and I think in Icelandic before finding the correct words in English.

The tourists on the bus are all older than me, in their 50s and 60s, curious about my stay here. They rave about my courage to learn the language and study in Iceland. Our first stop is Hveragerði, famous for its greenhouses. The weather is sunny and clear. I wonder if these folks realize how lucky they are to get such pleasant weather.

I'm interested in the vegetable greenhouses in Hveragerði, heated by hot water from volcanic springs. We stop at a Nesti for refreshments, and I cross the road to take some close-ups of a traditional Icelandic-style house with a rounded roof covered in sod. We visit the Kerið Volcanic Crater, where I walk the entire circumference with breathtaking views. I'm getting the reputation for being the most energetic on the trip. I think it's because I'm the youngest.

The tour continues to Skálholt, where I learn that It served as a key political and cultural center for eight centuries. I'm starting to get better acquainted with the others on the tour, a man from Copenhagen and couples from New Hampshire and Long Island.

The guide tells us that lunch will cost extra. I skip the meal and sit outside on a bench along the hillside to eat the sandwiches I brought. Then I stroll around the little village, enjoying my independence. When I return, the others from the tour are taking photos of a young girl in her Icelandic national costume. I'm surprised to see them tipping her, something not typically done here.

One of the women has purchased a package of Icelandic *harð-fiskur* (dried fish) as a snack. I've seen many folks here eat it, especially young kids in their strollers, chomping away at it like it's candy. This woman makes it look so appealing that I dash inside the shop to purchase a bag. I pull to break a piece off with my teeth. The texture is tough and chewy, like beef jerky. The taste is undeniably like salty, dried fish.

We visit Gullfoss (Golden Falls), one of Iceland's most popular and impressive waterfalls. It gets its name from the way the sunlight hits the water on a sunny day. The height doesn't distinguish Gullfoss from other waterfalls, but rather its great width. The couple from New Hampshire tell me how they envy my sturdy hiking boots and my high energy level. The couple is worn out after a ten-minute walk. If this trip were with the Icelandic Touring Club, I would be the one envying the others' excellent equipment and high energy level.

Our tour guide warns us about the danger of walking below the falls. The woman from Long Island tells me to be careful since she knows I'm determined to walk down below. The great span of the falls is breathtaking as I breathe in the drops of heavy spray gushing out from the falls. The day is so clear that we have an excellent view of Langjökull Glacier.

We drive on to the Great Geysir. The guide tells us this is the world's most famous geyser because this is the one all geysers are named after. Although the Great Geysir has stopped spewing, the nearby Strokkur Geysir remains the most active in the country. We enjoy seeing it erupt several times, as it sets off every four to ten minutes.

Finally, we reach Þingvellir National Park. The sunlight is disappearing with the start of some rain showers. The tour guide points out a wishing river, clear and deep and full of coins, so I add one Icelandic *króna* and make a wish that the rest of my stay in Iceland will bring more bright rainbows.

We make another stop at a shop for provisions, and I feel well looked after by the New Hampshire couple who share their chocolate chip cookies with me. I use my Icelandic to help one of the men on the tour get his change. I had told Svandís we'd be back at six, only we're 45 minutes late. I feel bad to have kept dinner waiting, especially because Birgir must leave for work at eight. It feels good to be back to what's now more normal for me, speaking Icelandic rather than English.

For my next excursion, I'm unsure whether I should go to the Snæfellsnes Peninsula or the Hekla Volcano. I call the Icelandic Touring Club and learn that the Hekla trip has been canceled. That settles it. I'll go to Snæfellsnes. I read that Snæfellsnes is called "Iceland in miniature" because of its wide range of landscapes, including the glacier that sits over a volcano on the peninsula's tip.

We are about to depart when I notice Svandís is still watching to see my bus leave. This touches my heart since this is something my dad would do. I think how this trip is going to be quite different from the one to Þórsmörk and the one I just took to Hveragerði, Gullfoss, and Þingvellir, with a larger busload of 43 travelers. I start a conversation with the woman sitting beside me on the bus. She points out the names of each mountain as we drive past. We stop at the Nesti at Hvalfjörður, where I buy a package of throat lozenges for my lingering sore throat. The weather is a drizzly rain. When we make a stop two hours later, the sun has come out again.

The tour guide announces over the microphone, Be sure to have your sunglasses, plenty of energy food, and liquids. Once again, I realize I've been totally in the dark about this trip. Not until the tour guide gives his instructions do I learn that we're not only going to admire the view, but we're going to climb Snæfellsnes Glacier! Since I didn't translate the written description of the tour word for word, I must have missed the part about climbing the 1,446-meter-high glacier. I'm unsure whether I'm more nervous or excited about climbing it. I think I would prefer jumping across the narrow blue rivers and the expansive green grass on the ground level rather than hiking up the slippery slope of the glacier.

We have to wait outside the Snæfellsnes shelter while the guide goes to collect the key. Several hiking groups have already set up their tents at a camp just outside the shelter. Once the door is opened and I look around, I discover we will be sleeping directly on the floor since the shelter has no bunk beds or mattresses.

The woman I sat beside on the bus lays out her sleeping bag to the right of mine. A hard-breathing man puts his sleeping bag on the other side, using the Icelandic *innsog* inhaling method, repeatedly saying *Já* (yes) and *Jaeja* (well) to himself. All the tour participants are eating the provisions they brought. The shelter doesn't provide any cookware or utensils, so I can't make tea.

I'm trying to figure out how to dress for tomorrow's climb. I watch the others lay out their fancy equipment with expensive hiking boots, hiking sticks, wool socks, and winter underwear. I also need to decide which provisions to bring along. Now I know just how unprepared I am without any liquids to carry on the hike. I'll have to make do with what I have: apples, oranges, and sandwiches.

Just before we head out the following morning, the woman who slept on the floor beside me decides to stay behind. She is my savior since she offers to loan me her sunglasses. We pass a few tents as we begin our ascent. I'm making mental notes about better equipment to bring whenever I go hiking again. Helga, a woman from the bus ride whom I've befriended, comments on how short the distance to the top looks. When the guide says the climb will take all day, I think the distance must be deceiving.

Each step involves lifting our feet through at least four inches of snow. I get incredibly thirsty and take to eating the snow. When I've eaten quite a large amount, a girl behind me tells me, You shouldn't eat the snow because it contains so much salt that it will make you sick. Another climber clarifies this, If you eat the snow when you're dehydrated, your stomach needs to melt the snow, which might make you sick. Either way, I stop eating the snow.

My shoes are getting sopping wet, and the water is soaking straight through my socks to my feet. Several hikers have noticed the wet stains on my brown leather hiking boots. They give me disapproving looks as they inquire about my wet feet. I don't let on how miserable it feels.

The sun has come out, and sweat has started to drip down my face and back. I had worried that I would freeze since everyone is warmly dressed. As we progress upwards, the others are stripping off their layers. Some women strip all the way down to their bras. Gradually, I take off my ski jacket and sweater, switching between the two at various intervals.

We stop to rest. I need these breaks to build up the strength and energy to continue. I watch thirstily, hungrily, and enviably as everyone else snacks on their chocolate, raisins, water, and juice. Helga generously offers to share some of her chocolate. Only eating the chocolate makes me even thirstier. I'm dreaming of gulping down gallons of ice-cold water.

We continue to embark on the steep, treacherous climb. This is not what I had in mind regarding sightseeing around the peninsula. I was picturing a leisurely tour with pleasant views. Not a steep hike requiring major hiking equipment, provisions, and even climbing rope. With each step of the upward climb, I feel so exhausted that I can barely lift my feet out of the snow. I have no choice but to keep going. The entire backside of my turtleneck is drenched in sweat.

I make small talk with Helga and three other women who are climbing in front of me. By late afternoon we approach the top. I'm in awe of the view of the clouds covering the blue sky and reflecting on the spotless white shiny glacier. Now, we still have to reach the high peak. My entire body is shaking, and I'm terrified. This is the first time I have experienced a fear of heights. To get to the top of the highest peak, I have to crawl over the snow on my knees, hanging onto the climbing rope as tight as I can to prevent falling and dying. When I finally reach the highest peak, I smile at the irony of climbing a 1,446-meter-high glacier without any intention of doing this.

My dry mouth is utterly thankful when one of the friendly ladies offers me her last sip of Icelandic moss tea. Even while surrounded by the glacial ice, the emotional ice has melted a bit as the other hikers are gracious and looking out for me. Another woman is my guardian angel since she supplies me with a fresh pair of dry wool socks. Getting a scolding from her for coming unprepared and inappropriately dressed is the price of the loan. I would be much more comfortable with the perfect hiking boots, clothing, and provisions. I console myself by acknowledging that having the ideal equipment requires prior guidance and knowledge.

Once I reach the top of the highest peak, I'm exhausted. All I want to do is trek back down as quickly as possible and return to the shelter. Instead, I'm reminded that the glacier has a twin peak. I noticed it on the way up but concentrated my efforts on reaching the highest peak. Little did I know that the Icelandic Touring Club motto is to *climb every mountain*! I can tell the second peak isn't as high, so I know it won't be as much of a struggle. Now I'm committed to climbing it with two ladies joining me. Giving in to this is a way to avoid making the trek down alone. All my muscles ache, but I'm thrilled to be on top of this snowy, icy white glacier. I see vibrant colors surrounding me: the crusty, white snow-covered glacier, the North Atlantic ocean a deep aqua blue, the mountains a rich navy blue, and the sunset a perfect blood orange.

Once we've climbed the second peak, I decide this was all worth it. This breathtaking view has made up for any misgivings and fed my hunger to see more of Iceland. I feel fully satisfied that I completed the climb to the top of both peaks.

We don't begin the trek down until nine in the evening. Compared to the slow speed on the way up, I'm nearly running to reach the bottom. The tour leader tells us, You were fortunate with the weather, making the snow conditions ideal for hiking. Many people come to climb the glacier without ever actually seeing it. His comments remind me of the fog and lack of visibility at Þórsmörk. I'm astonished to learn that one of the guides cross-country skied up and down the glacier five times during my one climb.

Back inside the warmth of the shelter, it feels glorious to sit down and rest my feet. One of the women in our group tells me, It feels as if I've just ridden a horse about 40 kilometers. I couldn't agree more.

I'm relieved to be able to drink the tap water from the shelter sink. Then I drink cold soup from my empty yogurt cup, using my knife as a spoon. I don't care about anything right now except going to sleep.

In the morning, I hear the others getting ready to begin another day of hiking. At least today, we'll be trekking on level ground, covering all the peninsulas, points, and coves. My legs ache from yesterday's climb, but I have no option other than to keep moving in the line.

The excitement for today is to see the Icelandic puffins. The tour guide explains that Iceland has an estimated population of eight to ten million puffins. I think back to how the guide at Gullfoss warned us how dangerous it was to walk down to the falls, and I did it without any trouble. Yet here, the guide gives no warning about any potential danger, even when I slip and scare myself. The others are more experienced hikers and continue without difficulty.

I'm thinking how generous and friendly the folks are on this tour. One of the women loans me her binoculars, bringing the puffins much closer to me. Through the binoculars, I see a seal colony and a small boat wreck that occurred just the night before. Further on, I'm intrigued as we peer into one of the rescue houses for shipwrecked sailors or stranded travelers, stocked with dry food, warm clothing, and sleeping bags.

The guide tells us about the four large stones on the black beach, each larger than the next. Those who succeed in lifting the heaviest and setting it up on the ledge prove their strength and vitality. Three men in our group lift the second heaviest 100 kilo stone. No one can lift the heaviest one at 154 kilos.

I watch the rest of the group enjoy their sandwiches and delicacies during the lunch break while I have nothing left except plain bread. We move on to see more cliffs, lava, and birds. My fellow hikers are taking photos with such impressive cameras and telephoto lenses that I feel inadequate with my basic-lensed Ricoh and pocket-sized Minolta. Helga and I take a strenuous walk over lava and hills at the last stop. I'm exhausted when we finally return to the shelter and barely have a chance to lie down before falling asleep.

After a two-hour nap, I awaken from deep sleep to hear singing and joke-telling in the shelter's larger wing. I join in to play the telephone game where one person whispers a phrase or a name into the ear of the person beside them, and then the words are passed around the circle. One round starts with the name *Snæfellsnes Jökull* (Glacier). When it reaches the end of the circle, the name comes out as *Marias Björnsson*, a made-up name. As I drift off to sleep, I overhear the women near me gossiping, including a mention of me. I'm too tired to pay any attention.

We start hiking early the next day on the path that borders the edge of the coastal cliffs. All 43 of us follow the tour guide in a line along the wet, green grass. After a few hours, I've had enough of jumping over the multitude of puddles, and I'm glad we return to the shelter. We pack up, empty all the trash, and scrub the floor so we'll leave the shelter cleaner than we found it. On the drive back, we stop in the small village of Buðír to hike some more coastal cliffs. As we head back to Reykjavík, three of the youngest boys in the group provide some entertainment on the bus by singing and telling jokes. My stomach starts acting up, becoming so bloated that I need to grab onto the seat cushion to handle the bumps in the road. My entire body starts to boil from a series of irrepressible cramps.

During the ride, I learn from Helga that the Icelandic Touring Club has been around for over 25 years. The club travels to Snæfell-snes annually, and many long-term members have climbed every peak and mountain in Iceland. Now that we've reached the bus station in Reykjavík, my stomach is still bloated in pain. I can't even walk straight, bending over as I struggle along since my stomach feels four feet wide. I head to a payphone to call Svandís. Helga interrupts and offers me a ride. All the hikers say their goodbyes, and I'm thinking, what a quick way to make 43 new friends.

I'm so happy to see Svandís and Birgir when they return to the apartment. It turns out that they had gone to pick me up at the bus station but missed me. When Svandís sees my new glacier-air suntan, she says, You don't need to go to Mallorca. You already have a tan. Dinner is a tender grilled lamb that tastes scrumptious since I've gone without a cooked meal the entire weekend. My stomach still aches unbearably, and I want to tell someone since I'm in need of sympathy. Svandís thinks I might be experiencing menstrual cramps. I have to tell her that I haven't had my period since I've been in Iceland. We discuss that this might be due to the change in diet and climate or anxiety. She comes to my room with a glass of 7-Up, just what I need for my dry throat and stomachache. We Icelandic kiss goodnight, and I think how special she is.

During my stay in Iceland, Ásta kept offering that she and Jón would show me around the country. She insisted we had to wait until the weather was better. With school out, I was impatient and wondered what to do. Sit and knit until the weather improved? I knew that travel at this time of year was taking a risk, and the weather did hamper my trip to Þórsmörk.

Looking back at how much I wanted to expand my travel knowledge of Iceland, these tours provided me with greater knowledge of the country. They helped me become more self-reliant. I learned what equipment and provisions I should have brought along and how to climb a glacier. I also learned to interact with other travelers. These tours helped build the momentum for my further travel around the world. Now when I plan a trip, I closely examine all aspects of the weather, the schedule, the packing, and exactly what the trip will entail, ensuring a fruitful and successful trip. Like the Icelandic proverb "a raisin at the end of a hotdog," I found that even a trip with bad weather, an unknown destination, the wrong equipment, or the wrong provisions is often still worth taking.

CHAPTER 11

Voyage Around Iceland

"Kemur allt með kalda vatninu."
Literal Meaning: It all comes with the cold water.
Intended Meaning: Good things come to those who wait.

My final hurrah in Iceland is embarking on a cargo ship around the country's coastline. Tourists rarely travel by cargo ship. Even more rarely does a young foreign girl of seventeen travel the whole ring. I owe this opportunity to Birgir, who works for Iceland customs at the Reykjavík shipyard and knows the ship's captain.

This trip is my consolation prize. My stay in Iceland is considered a stopover on my roundtrip fare to Luxembourg. The stopover has lasted close to a year. Before returning to Wisconsin, I dreamed of traveling to Luxembourg. However, Ásta and Jón can't find it in their reasoning for a young girl to travel alone to mainland Europe. In turn, the president of the Rotary Club of Iceland has denied me permission. This is the case, even when my parents sent a telegram giving their written consent.

I realize Ásta and Jón have begun to think of me as their daughter and don't want any harm to come to me. I don't want to do something against their wishes or jeopardize my relationship with them.

So, instead of traveling to Luxembourg, I'm circling the entire country of Iceland by ship. This means passing through majestic fjords with long hours of spring daylight. At every stop, I'll have

the chance to hop off the ship and roam the port towns at my lei-
sure. While on board, I can join the captain on the top deck to view
the shoreline and mingle with the crew and other passengers who
board for shorter voyages. I'm disappointed that I was denied my
first choice, but I found an excellent compromise. I'm excited to see
more of Iceland by traveling its circumference, especially when it
isn't typical for passengers to make this voyage.

It's May 23, and my first glimpse of the Esja cargo ship makes
my heart beat faster. Reality hits that I'll be traveling on board this
little beauty and seeing much more of Iceland during this one-week
voyage. Once on board, a young crew woman named Hildur, shows
me to my cabin. While tiny and sparse, it's nicer than I imagined.
The cabin is a cozy space with a dark brown wooden interior, including built-in bunk beds, a desk, a radio, a sink, and a tiny, square
porthole window. Unlike at Bifröst, the bathroom and shower are
across the narrow hallway from my cabin.

Birgir introduces me to the captain while we sip coffee in the
ship's dining room. The captain is short with a round, jolly face
in his late 50s. His dark-rimmed glasses give him a studious look,
while his leathery-skinned face reveals the years he's spent at sea.
The captain smiles as he explains how his crewmen were delighted
to learn that a teenage girl would be a passenger for the entire route.
My enthusiasm about the adventure makes it challenging to concentrate on Birgir's explanation of the other ships the captain has
commanded.

The captain explains that this ship is named after Mt. Esja, the
volcanic mountain that serves as a backdrop to Reykjavík. It was
built in 1967 in Akureyri to carry everyday household items such
as food, clothing, and building materials to all ports of Iceland. The
ship has a total of 21 cabins, including 15 for crewmembers and six
for passengers.

As Esja departs the Reykjavík harbor, I wave goodbye to Birgir from the deck. The bright sunshine allows for the best shots I've ever taken of Reykjavík.

Inside the ship's small but elegant wood-lined dining room, a filling dinner of fish and potatoes is followed by a hot, syrupy blueberry soup and a strong cup of coffee. I speak in Icelandic with the two other passengers on board, a mother and daughter returning home to Ísafjörður. They are shocked to learn I'll be traveling on Esja for the entire voyage. The mother tells me, I can't imagine anyone circling the whole country by cargo ship, just for fun. The mother and daughter take pills to prevent seasickness while the table sways back and forth, moving us with it.

I'm curious about all the nooks and crannies on the ship, only I'm cautious about wandering around since I haven't been invited to explore much. I head up to the top deck above the captain's bridge, where I stare at the sea. I feel less sick to my stomach if I stare directly ahead at the waves rather than sitting on the lower deck or inside my cabin. I prefer to see where we're headed.

The captain startles me when he comes up behind me and shouts, It isn't safe sitting up on this deck like that! I move to the lower deck just above my cabin level, facing the side, then soon head downstairs to the bathroom. On my way back upstairs, I pass the head crewman, Ragnar, in the narrow hallway. From his face, I can tell something is wrong.

He says, The captain has been looking for you.

I think, but I only went to the bathroom!

He's afraid you've fallen in.

I feel bad for having caused such worry. I can't help inventing another imaginary news headline: Wisconsin Girl Lost At Sea Trying To See More Of Iceland.

The crewman warns me, Never go up on the top deck alone! Then how am I to get good photos? I'll have to be satisfied with taking pictures from the lower deck unless someone permits me to go to the top.

When I do return to the top deck, I make sure someone else is there as I excitedly snap photos of the Snæfellsnes Glacier I climbed just a week earlier. Seeing the glacier and the impressive cliffs on the peninsula takes my breath away, temporarily removing any thought of seasickness. However, nausea sets in as soon as I return to my cabin. I try writing in my journal but can't look down without feeling sick. Sleeping is not an option. I return to the lower deck to take in the sunset while the expansive glacier remains in the forefront. It's nearly midnight. I decide not to change into my pajamas in case I need to dash upstairs for more photo opportunities.

Every hour, I wake up a little nauseous and peek out my tiny square porthole to ensure I'm not missing any significant scenery. Over the ship's loudspeaker, Ragnar announces breakfast and updates us on the rough weather we're experiencing. As I open the door to the dining room, Hildur asks, Were you seasick during the night? To save my pride, I say, *Nei, nei,* which is just a slight fib.

My imagination runs wild when I am the only guest for breakfast, with a single place setting and fine china on a white tablecloth. The formality of the server and the elegance of the table, make me picture myself in a movie. I imagine that I'm a detective in a murder mystery, attempting to solve the case.

Luckily, the weather has turned clear. Esja is sailing so smoothly that it feels as stable as if we were on land. As Esja arrives at the entrance to Ísafjarðardjúp, my first opportunity to sail through an Icelandic fjord begins. I'm overcome with the feeling of freedom from escaping Bifröst. At the same time, the snowy mountains surrounding the ship on each side offer a comforting snugness. I'm impressed with how the snow hugs the mountain crevices, creating artistic patterns that resemble Matisse cut-outs.

We arrive at Isafjörður, the capital of the Westfjords region. The captain announces that we'll be here for five hours. Isafjörður is the largest settlement in the area, with a population of about 3,000. I have no way to disguise that I'm a stranger as my face burns red from the townspeople's heavy stares. Once I've covered the entire ring of the town, I enter a small shop to buy a postcard and then sit on a park bench to write to my family. I head over to the post office to mail it. Even with all the stares, I feel a rush of independence to be here on my own. What a stark contrast to how locked in I felt the last four months.

Upon returning to the ship, I'm pleased to discover that the ship has housekeeping service. My room is all tidy, and my bed has been made. The cook informs me that lunch is ready, potato soup followed by Hungarian goulash. When I'm done, I head back to town to find the streets entirely empty. All the stores are closed since everyone has gone home for lunch.

I walk up the hillside to a small farm where a herd of fluffy white sheep and hundreds of lambs are grazing, plus several geese and ducks are honking. Two young boys call out to me and I make their acquaintance as they ask me my name and I learn theirs. I finish my snack of biscuits and a chocolate bar while sitting at the same park bench as earlier. I visit the maritime museum, followed by the town library, where I read an article about Prince Charles in *Time* magazine. I take one last stroll around town, thinking how strange it is to have exhausted everything to do in Isjafjörður in one day while others spend their whole lives here.

I'm finding the crewmembers place a lot of emphasis on meal-times. Hildur and the captain inform me that *kaffi* is ready and insist that I not miss it. Once again, I'm worried about the quantity and heaviness of the food. I head to the dining hall for cookies and raisin bread and chat with the two female kitchen workers, Guðrún and Kristín. A crewman named Sigurður, with broad, muscular shoulders, asks me, How did you like Isafjörður? Did you meet any boys? In addition to mealtime, romantic prospects are a favorite topic among the crew.

That evening, we make an unexpected stop at Bolungarvík, one of Iceland's oldest fishing outposts. Bolungarvík reminds me of Isafjörður, except smaller. It feels remarkable to sightsee in these untouristed, out-of-the-way places. I window shop in a few closed stores, again receiving some hard stares from the townspeople. It must be strange to them when I disappear just as quickly as I've appeared.

When I return to the ship, the captain asks, Did you have a chance to see Bolungarvík? He's concerned that I'm bored. I assure him that I'm not.

Then Hildur asks, Do you want to be awakened when we pass Hornbjarg, an enormous cliff in the Westfjords?

Of course!

At three in the morning, I hear Hildur's knock as we're passing Hornbjarg, one of the northernmost locations in Iceland. I step out on the lower deck to take in the view. Even at this hour, there is still some twilight. The captain explains how the cliffs are known for their unusual shape, giving them the appearance of a cresting wave. I'm relieved to view Hornbjarg from the ship rather than attempting to walk the rugged cliff edges.

The morning sunshine peering in through the porthole wakes me. I jump out of bed, into my clothes, and up to the bridge. I'm delighted to get a clear view of Drangey, a small island in the center of Skagafjörður, the remnant of a 700,000-year-old volcano. The island is home to 350,000 puffins and many other seabirds. Unfortunately, none of these are possible to see today.

The captain relates an Icelandic tale to me about a famous outlaw, Grettir Ásmudarson, who lived on Drangey Island. As the saga goes, Grettir was known to be bad-tempered but also the loveable son of a Viking. He was responsible for a hall fire that killed several men and forced him into hiding. The captain tells me that Grettir escaped with his brother and hid on the island for 20 years until he was caught by his enemies and killed on one of Drangey's rocky cliffs.

We pass more long green, grassy fjords. I'm offered coffee and conversation while the captain shows me the remaining route on the map. He's mentioned several times how lucky we've been with the weather. He tells me, I'll have to take you along on every voyage to ensure the weather will be this good.

As soon as I'm done with lunch, I head straight to the top deck to get a view of Siglufjörður, one of the northernmost towns in Iceland. I glimpse the Olafsfjörður fishing village and spot the island of Hrisey through my binoculars. Just as we're passing the small town of Dalvík, I overhear the captain shouting in fiery red-hot Icelandic at one of the young crewmen, Stay away from the edge!

When I take a closer look at the crewmen, I notice that quite a few doing the heavy lifting are young teenagers. The cook teases one of the young crewmen about "having a party" since he has me to look at. When I see several of the young shirtless crewmen, with droplets of sweat glistening on their broad shoulders, I think it's as much a pleasure for me.

I've been to Akureyri before, but I still enjoy playing tourist. I purchase a few postcards, revisit the landmark church, and then the city parks. I call Glen, the other Rotary exchange student in Iceland this year, to plan a time to meet up. He's focused on arranging some work and weekend home stays before he heads to Luxembourg. It still bothers me that Glen has received permission to travel to Luxembourg while I have not.

Glen and I sit at a park bench and share stories. I'm comforted to know he is also experiencing homesickness. Glen asks if his friend can use my plane ticket to Luxembourg since I'm not allowed to go. Well, I guess I'm glad someone else will be able to use it.

I take a swim at the public geothermal heated swimming pool. How liberating to swim several laps in the lusciously warm, steaming water. Then I rush down the steps into the even hotter and more soothing, circular hot pool. Following my luxurious swim, I plan to go to the movie theater. I'm excited as this is my first opportunity to go to a movie alone. The passage on the cargo ship has given me the thrill of going where I want, when I want, without having to consult with anyone other than the captain to check how long we'll be at each port.

After a pleasant night's slumber, I head out for another busy day in Akureyri. First, I buy two Icelandic pottery dishes at the tourist bureau and pick up some tourist pamphlets. I'm irritated because the girl in the tourist office speaks English to me. She couldn't know I prefer to speak Icelandic. Then I buy some envelopes in a shop next door. Once again, the shopkeeper speaks to me in English. Naturally, they expect to speak English with foreigners stopping in. I head back up the church steps to the bench where I sat yesterday with Glen. I'm happy to sit alone, soaking up the peace and solitude. The trees are short and stubby but also bright spring green. Looking down the hillside at the blue bay, the vibrant purple lupines make for a remarkable sight.

I return to Esja for another hearty lunch. The captain comes into the dining room to inform me, It's raining cats and dogs in Reykjavík! He adds, We're lucky we have the weather we have here in Akureyri.

When I head out, I decide to give myself the luxury of not knowing my destination. On my way, I meet up with the cook from the ship, who asks if we can walk together. He tells me he's on his way to the swimming pool. He makes small talk, comparing Iceland to the United States and how Americans have it so good. He says, Icelanders are only interested in making money and buying cars. That's all they talk about.

Following this conversation, I end up back at the bench in the park and savor one last panoramic view of Akureyri.

When I return to my cabin, the noise of the ship workers pounding away outside my cabin window makes it difficult to rest. I still manage to fall asleep. I awaken to feel the ship moving as we leave port. I rush up on deck to see Akureyri disappear.

Sigurður sees me looking over the sketches of the ship. He asks, Do you want to see the engine room? *Sure*, I answer. He gives me a set of earplugs as we head down the narrow, inner steps to the engine room. In the lower office, Sigurður explains the machinery and devices. We talk about my stay here in Iceland. He says, You must have studied Icelandic before you came to Iceland since you speak it so correctly.

We arrive in Húsavík, the oldest settlement in Iceland, at close to midnight. The captain tells me we'll be here for two hours. The sky is still not completely dark, only it's not light enough to take photos. I'm determined to get a firsthand look at the town. I see the old wooden church built in 1907, the main store, the nursing home, a school, and a small hotel. Two cars keep passing me, one full of boys and the other full of girls, making me uneasy. It must look odd for a young stranger to show up in town at midnight on a Friday night. Húsavík is so tiny that I can circle the entire town in half an hour. A dusty blue jeep passes me several times and disappears into the distance. I head back to the harbor and onboard Esja, into my cabin, onto the lower bunk bed, thoroughly tired, and fall straight asleep.

We arrive at Raufarhöfn in the morning, one of the northern-most towns in Iceland (along with Siglufjörður, which we stopped at earlier). From the top deck, I see a tiny fishing village with little to explore. I embark to take a look anyway. The captain tells me they'll be done loading by noon. I overhear that they have 60 tons to load, so it's doubtful they'll finish by then.

Here too, all the drivers and passengers in the cars turn their heads to stare as they pass by. I walk around the peninsula to get a view across the harbor and take a photo looking back at the ship. I return for lunch, which is fish and potatoes again. The bread soup for dessert is a bit lumpy and doesn't taste as good as Ásta's. Afterward, I retire to my cabin to read, which turns into a nap until I wake up feeling the ship leaving port, so I head up to the bridge. Shortly after *kaffi*, we arrive at Þórshöfn. I head out to cover a ring around the town.

As I wander along the gravel road, a female voice shouts from behind me, *Pála!* I'm wondering how anyone could know me here. It turns out to be Líney, one of the second-year students from Bifröst. How extraordinary to bump into her. She says she recognized my ski jacket as I passed by her window. Then she rushed out on her brother's bike to catch up to me.

Líney invites me to her home. I'm worried the ship might leave without me, but I accompany her up the hill to her house for a short visit. Upstairs, I meet her mother, who works at the post office, her two brothers, and her two grandmothers. Líney sets out crackers and bread while her mother boils eggs and shells shrimp to serve as a salad with tea. I'm enjoying the visit but still feeling stressed that the ship might leave. The shrimp salad tastes delicious, and the time passes quickly as we chat away.

We rush back down the hill together to reach the port by six. One of the younger ship crewmen passes by and does a doubletake when he sees me talking with Líney, wondering how I could know anyone here. Ragnar tells me that the ship will be here until nine, so I make plans to meet Líney after dinner.

Líney and her family are still eating when I return. Both of Líney's grandmas are at the table, telling her, Líney do this, Líney do that. I didn't know her very well at Bifröst. It's taken this unexpected encounter at the opposite end of the country to learn more about her.

Líney's mom is making a black-backed gull egg for me. At least, that's what she tells me it is, not that I've ever come across one before. I'm a little scared as I watch her prepare it, realizing that I will have to eat this enormous black and blue speckled egg which they consider a delicacy. I use my spoon to break into the thick eggshell to discover that the egg white is transparent and rubbery. It tastes delicious despite its unappetizing appearance.

We sit and watch a British TV special featuring John Lennon, Peter Sellers, Julie Andrews, and Tom Jones. I chat with Líney's mom, and she compliments me on my Icelandic. Líney puts on a record album she bought in Mallorca on the student trip. She shows me a white rabbit fur jacket with leather trim that she purchased on the trip and that I've fallen in love with. She tells me, Everything was so inexpensive in Mallorca compared to Iceland, so I bought two leather purses, two pairs of leather boots, leather clogs, and two gauze blouses!

If I don't return to Esja in time, Líney's mom assures me they will drive me to Vopnafjörður to meet the ship. This still doesn't calm my nerves, so Líney gives me a ride down to the harbor. I relax when we see the crew still working away. I ask Líney if she knows everyone in town, and she says, Yes, every single person. That's difficult for me to imagine. Líney's interested in having a look onboard Esja, and I feel lucky to have the opportunity to show a friend around. We watch TV in the ship lounge, and she tells me more about her Mallorca trip. Eventually, Líney needs to leave to return the jeep to her dad.

During breakfast, I sit with a 75-year-old passenger who has just come aboard the night before. He is tall, slender, and stately looking in his tweed suit. He gives me a friendly smile and then does a lot of talking to himself. I'm not sure if he's hard of hearing or if it's my poor Icelandic. He can't seem to follow what I say.

When we arrive in foggy, rainy Vopnafjörður, I realize how much the weather affects my impression of these port towns. This one doesn't appear to be anything special in the rain. I walk the streets while gripping my jacket tails, trying to stay warm. Ásta told me her brother lives here. I look around at the houses, wondering which one is his.

Our next stop is Bakkaferði in East Borgarfjarðar. I'm delighted to disembark in the bright sunshine and walk down a path to observe a fishing boat with the fishermen at work. One of the fishermen shouts to me, You shouldn't take any more photos, or you'll break your camera. This makes me smile.

I see the fish drying racks and then notice the sails. Another one of the fishermen yells out to me in English, Where are you from?

I say in Icelandic, I'm an exchange student from the United States.

You're going on a ring trip?

Yes.

Not seasick?

No. I'm proud to say.

I rush back onboard Esja to change my film. While I take a photo from the harbor pier, my lens cap is picked up by the wind and heads straight into the bay. From the deck, I wave to the fishermen I photographed just moments before, while the breeze blows across my windburned face.

The waves have grown to their roughest so far on the voyage. The four new passengers we picked up in East Borgarfjarðar are now all seriously seasick, something I've managed to avoid. Dinner is the same as lunch. This time it doesn't agree with my stomach and it's the closest I've come to throwing up. We arrive in Seydisfjörður at eight in the evening. I'm the first to disembark as soon as the gangplank is set in place.

I awake at two in the morning to discover we've just made port in Norðfjörður. I head up to the bridge to scope out the town through Jón's binoculars. The captain asks, Were you awakened by the waves? I hate to admit it, indeed, I was. The captain shouts out orders to the crew to prepare for departure. Back in my cabin, the waves have become rougher, making me nauseated, so I return to the bridge to sit with the captain. At four, I go back to my cabin and sleep until the morning breakfast call.

The elderly gentleman is already seated at breakfast. We dock at Eskifjörður, and as I head out, he says to me, It's a lovely sunny day for picture taking.

That is precisely what I intend to do. I discover a tall, flowing waterfall with some sheep grazing alongside it and think what a picturesque, peaceful town. I meet up with the gentleman from the ship. If I speak louder, he seems to understand my Icelandic better. We have a lengthy conversation about a large, wooden, unusual-looking building and wonder what it might be used for. With his round, bald head, great curiosity, and gift for conversation, he reminds me of my grandfather. I hear him relaying our story about the mysterious-looking building to one of the crewmen back on board.

We travel the short distance from Eskifjörður to reach Reðarfjörður, where I spot a long crew boat filled with bare-shouldered, muscular young men paddling past. The elderly gentleman explains to me that they're training to become seamen. I rush up on deck to take their photo while they wave back and cheer at me.

As we reach Reðarfjörður, I ask the captain my usual question, *Hvað lengi* (How long)? He tells me, One hour. I make my way from the harbor up the hill to the town. Walking along the water, I pass the same boat of male rowers. They stare and size me up and down. I'm wondering, haven't they ever seen a girl before?

I stop at the post office to mail an aerogram. Then I walk around town searching for any traces of the naval base from World War II that I've heard about. I discover the Icelandic Wartime Museum, but I don't have enough time to visit it. As I enter the town grocery store, I discover Bekka, a second-year student from Bifröst, standing behind the counter.

I greet her in formal Icelandic, *Komdu sæl* (hello), and she gives me a warm, surprised smile. We chat a bit, and now I feel I know more people in Iceland in the months I've been here than in all of Green Bay. I walk back to the ship whistling. Then I take a deep breath of the fresh air, trying to keep these fun memories safe in my heart.

Up on the bridge, I watch the view until we arrive in Fáskrúðs-fjörður, a tiny town on the east coast with about 100 inhabitants. The heavy rain doesn't make it a good stop for exploring or photography.

This is my first opportunity to observe the ship workers unloading goods. I'm wondering how they know precisely which crate to move. With the variability in cargo, it must be difficult to predict how long the loading and unloading will take at each port. Earlier, the captain told me we'd be here for half an hour, and now it's going on two hours. As we leave port, I watch the news on TV and listen to the crew tell their sea stories.

We land at Stöðvarfjörður, a tiny fjord and village on the eastern coast of Iceland which has the same population as the last port. I decide not to venture out in the freezing rain. A crewman tells me, You probably wished you'd stayed back at Fáskrúðsfjörður, now that the weather has turned rough.

A British espionage movie is on TV in the lounge area, helping me keep my mind off the severe weather. I watch from the bridge as Esja heads out of Stöðvarfjörður. One of the young, handsome crewmen keeps making faces at me, causing me to smile and laugh. Due to the upcoming treacherous weather, I overhear that we'll be skipping the next several fjords and heading straight to the town of Höfn to reach it by morning. The captain points out Höfn on the map for me, a small peninsula and one of the few harbors in the southeast. He tries to help me say the name "Höfn" since I find it difficult to pronounce. The best I can do is to try to say "hup" while inhaling. The captain warns me not to go outside on any deck alone tomorrow since the weather will be too rough. He tells me, It will still be all right for you to come up to the bridge if you like.

Just as the captain warned, the weather is getting consistently worse. The constant high waves and rocking of the ship are hard on my stomach, making it impossible to read or write. I try laying on my lower bunk bed. Lying flat leads to nausea, and I must sit back up immediately. This is the worst I've felt on Esja so far. I think my stomach is about to fall out of my body. It hurts my pride, but hard as I try, I can't prevent myself from throwing up in my cabin sink. What a putrid smell inside this tiny cabin. I don't want to stay in my cabin feeling nauseated and miserable, so I head up to the bridge at two in the morning to face questioning stares from the crew.

Sigurður takes one look at me and asks if I'm seasick. Rather than admit it, I tell him I couldn't sleep. It's more calming to stare straight ahead at sea rather than lying horizontal in bed. I'd rather face the crewmen's curious inquiries than suffer in my cabin.

The gale force winds are causing four-to-six-meter-high waves, and with each harsh hit, I hold on tight to avoid falling off the chair. The roughness and the nausea are scaring me. I fear the high waves will never stop. My stomach has a continual dropping feeling, and I need to hold onto it to prevent myself from throwing up again. I stare straight ahead at the blowing sea waves out the bridge windows. Then my eyes get so sleepy that I can't keep them open, so I return to my cabin at three in the morning. The captain confirmed that we'll arrive in Höfn by seven, and I intend to be awake for that.

Only I don't wake up until seven-thirty to discover we're still en route. The waves are still six meters high, and I'm upset that I can't prevent myself from throwing up, once again, all over my periwinkle windbreaker. I quickly wash it out and head back up to the bridge, where I find the captain. He informs me that we've only traveled eight miles in eight hours since the weather hasn't calmed down.

The captain calls the staff In Hornafjörður, the fjord we need to pass through to reach Höfn, to check whether the strong winds will require us to bypass it. The crew is relieved to learn that we are going to skip Höfn due to the stormy weather conditions. It looks as if we're in for a rough day.

During breakfast, Hildur informs me that the other two passengers onboard slept through the entire storm. If only I'd been that lucky. I head back to the bridge, where the captain hands me a certificate verifying that I reached the Arctic Circle at the northern-most part of our voyage.

I nearly throw up again from the smell of food coming from the kitchen. When I catch a glimpse of a seasick, sweating, half-dead-looking young crewman, my stomach is too uneasy, and I skip lunch. I return to my cabin and head straight to bed, thinking if the other passengers can sleep, I should be able to also.

Up from my afternoon nap just in time for *kaffi*. The powerful aroma of freshly baked bread makes me hungry, and I'm finally able to face food. I go straight up to the bridge afterward.

The storm has passed! Esja is surrounded by picturesque views of sea birds, islands, mountains, glaciers, and a school of whales swimming by. These views are accompanied by a colorful sunset, keeping me busy with my camera and binoculars, racing from one side of the bridge to the other. I take photos of the famous Reynis-drangar basalt sea stacks created thousands of years ago by volcanic activity. I see a hollow arch that boats pass under, and then I spot Vestmannaeyjar, surrounded by hundreds of fishing boats.

I'm excited as we near Vestmannaeyjar with the sun behind Surtsey and all the islands, forming a view I must photograph. The 75-year-old gentleman says, I've lived in Iceland all my life but never been to Vestmannaeyjar before, and here you are returning for your second visit!

I wonder if any of Birgir's relatives will be there to meet me when we dock. I don't expect them to since it's so late at night. Through Jón's binoculars, I see the familiar sight of the harbor with the smoking lava, the steep cliff, and the hovering seagulls. Then I spot Birgir's relatives, Anna and Elisabet, waving to me from the dock. I run down to my cabin to get my camera and gear. In the hallway, Ragnar says, Your friends have come for you.

I rush down the plank to greet them. Since there's not much visibility at this hour, I decide there's no point in taking any pho-tos. Instead, I enjoy the company of these two wide-awake women spoiling me with their attention. We sip coffee and munch on cookies, and I rattle on, bursting with stories about my circle trip.

Anna and Elisabet take me for a spin around the island, which is fun even in the dark, getting glimpses of the familiar sights from my previous visit at Easter. We return to the harbor just in time for the two o'clock departure. It's late for these two, especially Anna, who must start work in a few hours. We exchange Icelandic kisses, and I laugh when Anna says, The next time you return to Iceland, you might come with your husband and kids.

Back aboard Esja, a crew member kindly informs me that I should go to bed. I'm too excited to sleep, so I head up to the bridge, where Ragnar asks me how I liked Vestmannaeyjar. He's surprised to hear that I've been here before. Then he tells me that he's originally from Vestmannaeyjar and knows Elisabet, Anna, and Birgir. I head to the bridge to await cast-off. I get tired of waiting, and I return to my cabin. There's no possibility of going to sleep, so I climb the stairs back to the bridge, where my reappearance disturbs the captain and Ragnar.

Ragnar asks, Why aren't you going to sleep?

I say, The scenery is too good to miss by sleeping.

When I run out of film and my eyes start to feel heavy, I have no choice but to return to my cabin. With the morning daylight seeping in, I don't fall asleep until 4 a.m.

The aroma of freshly baked bread has become my morning alarm clock. I'm amazed how the cook can bake such delicious bread in such a tiny kitchen. The elderly gentleman joins me in the dining room, and we chat about Vestmannaeyjar. I'm taken aback when he pulls out a 5,000 *krónur* bill from his wallet (about $25 U.S.) and hands it to me. I'm sure he means well by this act of kindness, with his love of kids, including ten of his own, plus 70 grandkids. He says, I want to give this to you since you're so energetic with sightseeing and taking photos. The condition I make in accepting his generosity is to insist that he give me his name and address so I can send him a thank you in return.

As this is the final day of the voyage, I return to the bridge. The visibility is impaired by the heavy fog and rain. I catch hazy glimpses as we pass by Grindavík, Keflavík, and Sandgerði, and a distant view of a school of whales, as we near the Reykjavík harbor. The ship crew is painting the walls outside my cabin door. I come out to the deck to check the view and take photos. They whistle and ask, What do you see? I respond, The *same* thing as you. Perhaps the view is less intriguing to them when they've done the trip repeatedly.

As Esja approaches the Reykjavík harbor, I search for Birgir and Svandís through Jón's binoculars. I'm happy to spot their familiar faces here to greet me. All the kids are waving. The elderly gentleman tells me, That gives me such pleasure to see your friends have come to meet you.

I thank the captain and say, Maybe I'll come back someday. He adds, Perhaps with your husband. I laugh and then shake the cook's hand as he tells me, It was an exciting trip. Too bad it had to end.

——◇——

Looking back, I'm confident I could have traveled to Luxembourg since my Icelandic experience had already prepared me for it. Thinking about it now, it seems strange that my host parents didn't hesitate to send me to a boarding school where I was exposed to smoking, drinking, pornography, and a stranger in my bed. Or on a cargo ship full of young crewmen where I stopped at strange towns at all hours of the day and night. That Glen was allowed to go to Luxembourg while I was not, makes me shudder at the unconscious gender discrimination.

However, only two years later, I did travel to Luxembourg and since then have taken many trips around Europe. It's not likely I'll ever have the opportunity to take a cargo ship around Iceland again.

The consolation prize of traveling on a cargo ship around the country gave me the independence I sought after feeling stifled in the middle of nowhere at Bifröst. It was exciting to bump into acquaintances just by wandering onshore in out-of-the-way places. The circle voyage was an exceptional opportunity to admire Iceland's stark, natural beauty, providing me with far-reaching, lasting memories. I can still smell the warm fresh bread baking in the kitchen onboard Esja. I remember the kindness of the old gentleman passenger. Also, I remember the locals' curiosity as they stole glimpses of a young foreigner traipsing through their town for a few hours and then disappearing quickly. These are the memories of ice and rainbows that I carry with me and cherish.

CHAPTER 12

Running Out of Ice

"Að slá einhverjum gullhamra."
Literal meaning: To hit somebody with a golden hammer.
Intended meaning: Receiving a compliment can be a bit painful, despite the golden glow of it.

This is the last chapter of my stay in Iceland, at least for this year. I have a few more items to take care of before I'm ready to leave. Following all these months of studying the language, going to school, trying to fit in, and traveling around the country, I now have a chance to enjoy everyday life in Iceland. As luck would have it, I've returned to shore to "my favorite" dinner of boiled sheep's head. Svandís says, You took so little! I stick to the white meat and mix it thoroughly with the mashed potatoes to disguise the taste. During my stay in Iceland, I have found new foods that I consider delicious and a few that I've found to be nearly inedible.

Svandís serves prune soup for dessert. I've acquired a taste for this soup since I love the fruity flavor. I help Svandís with the dishes and confide in her my fear that I've put on weight. She tells me, You don't look any heavier than when you arrived in Iceland. I know she's trying to make me feel better. Perhaps she thought I already looked heavy when I arrived.

The subject of Greenpeace and saving the whales is covered during the evening news on TV, with a special report from the whale station at Hvalfjörður. The whale hunting season has begun again. On the program, an entire whale is dissected, which is just as disturbing to see televised as it was in person during stops at the station.

Birgir asks me to tell him more about my Esja voyage, so I describe my adventures in more detail. I tell him about the older gentleman on board who befriended me, the stops in the middle of the night at the various ports, and how wonderful it was that his relatives greeted me at Vestmannaeyjar. He tells me that he was sure I'd have an enjoyable experience on the Esja circle trip.

When I go for one final orthodontist appointment, I'm surprised when he tells me he'll remove my braces. It seems odd timing since my orthodontist in Green Bay could take them off in a few weeks. I'm still delighted at the prospect. The orthodontist impresses me with how he can conduct two conversations simultaneously—one with me and another with the two assistants in the other room. They seem so involved in their discussion, with me simply a patient to be worked on.

It feels wonderful to be liberated from these silver wires that have banded my teeth for two and a half years. I will need to learn how to talk through my new retainer. I'm delighted to look in the mirror and see my teeth smiling at me.

When Svandís picks me up, she tells me how good I look without the braces. We make the rounds to shop for new pants for Vigfus, Birgir Jón, and Ásta Margrét. I've found that shopping isn't that fun here in Iceland as the prices are incredibly high, without a wide variety to choose from.

We bump into Jói Bekk, one of the second-year students from Bifröst. Then, almost immediately, we encounter Elisabet, also from Bifröst. She has just returned from a trip to Luxembourg. I explain how I took a cargo ship around the country and ran into Bekka in Reyðarfjörður. I had no idea when she tells me that she is also from Reyðarfjörður. Bumping into all these acquaintances makes me feel more connected.

On the bus ride back to Borgarnes with Ásta Margrét the next day, we make the usual stop at the Nesti in Hvalfjörður, where we buy Cokes and Prince Polo chocolate bars. This might be my last Prince Polo during my stay in Iceland. Three German tourists are on the bus, and I smile overhearing them trying to converse with two Icelanders using a combination of German, English, and a few Icelandic words.

Jón greets us at the bus stop in Borgarnes. Ásta catches me up on the latest gossip in Borgarnes when finally, she notices my braces are gone, and then she compliments me on how much tanner and skinnier I look.

I spend the next day packing. Ásta keeps checking on me, worrying that I won't be able to fit everything in my luggage. Later that evening, the conversation turns again to how many children I plan to have. I explain that for what feels like the 100th time, I will not have any kids. This is followed by their standard response, You'll change your mind.

I'm pleased to switch topics and begin a discussion about pets, and I mention the parakeet my family used to have, plus gerbils and turtles. Then we talk about mosquitoes, tarantulas, and stink bugs, and Ásta tells me that the thought of all these bugs makes her afraid to visit the United States. This discussion brings up something unique about Iceland, it has no mosquitoes. While Iceland does have tiny flying midges, it has very few other bugs or flies. I ask why and Ásta and Jón explain that it's because of Iceland's unique weather conditions.

When I awaken the following day, Ásta tells me about the loud hailstorm during the night that kept them awake. I didn't hear a sound. The salmon Jón picked up for lunch is tender and delicious. The salmon soup, however, is difficult to swallow with such an intense salmon flavor and an unusual combination of sherry, prunes, and raisins. I'm dreaming of my return to Wisconsin when I'll be able to eat more green leafy vegetables and less starch, and what I want when I want.

That night, Ásta Margrét and Ásta talk about how I didn't know a single word of Icelandic when I arrived. We all laugh together since they've decided how I should respond to the customs officer at the airport if questioned about my suitcase full of a dozen hand-knit Icelandic sweaters. I'm to say, I spent a year in Iceland, and I've been knitting the entire time!

We head upstairs to enjoy the brilliant sunshine out on the patio. I remember seeing this view for the first time all those months ago and how different it looked from Wisconsin landscapes. As my adopted home away from home, the view has become a good friend to me. We say our goodnights with Icelandic kisses. I put on one of Árni's Beatles records and climb onto the sofa bed under the quilt. I can't sleep since my head is spinning with thoughts about returning home to Wisconsin, how sorry I am to leave Iceland, and wondering what I've missed for a year of school back home.

I wake up to discover I slept in once again. Even the bright daylight didn't wake me. Over breakfast, Ásta tells us how good the weather is for sunbathing. Ásta Margrét and I tape aluminum foil to the wood fence on the side of the house to enhance our tans. We look at each other and start laughing at the funny sight we must make. Here we are lying in our teeny-tiny bikinis that Ásta and Jón brought back for us from the Canary Islands, trying to get tans next to aluminum foil in 60-degree Fahrenheit weather.

When Jón returns from work, Ásta mixes the batter to make waffles topped with orange marmalade. Ásta is certain that the Borgarnes Rotary Club will give me a gift and worries how I'll fit it in my luggage. I have the butterflies as I dress for my last Rotary meeting in Iceland. Outside in the garden, Ásta inspects my outfit. She tells me, You look so fine.

Stepping inside the Borgarnes Hotel with Jón, I'm relieved when we're greeted with handshakes rather than Icelandic kisses from the elderly Rotary members. I'm led up front as the guest of honor and sit next to Magnús, the headmaster from Hvanneyri, who is also the Borgarnes Rotary president. I feel honored that they have come out tonight just because of me, switching their usual meeting night to see me off.

The Rotarians proceed through the usual meeting activities. I learn that Jón has been giving weekly reports on my whereabouts as the members know I've just returned from a cargo ship trip around Iceland.

Then Magnús introduces my Borgarnes English teacher, Guð-munder, who summarizes my contributions to the community. Even after all my efforts and protests to have folks speak Icelandic to me, I guess it should be expected that Guðmunder, the English teacher, would speak in English. He stands up and says, It's always the case that when we look back on something, we often feel as though we could have helped more. It is an Icelandic custom to give a gift, not that large, but that the friendship should stand for more than the gift.

Guðmunder presents me with a book of poems by famous Icelan-dic poets, shakes my hand, and thanks me. Hauker, the headmaster from Bifröst, stands up and acknowledges some of the struggles I've had to endure. He says, It was challenging to start at a new school in the middle of the school year, but she created interest in the students and got involved as much as could be expected for arriving midyear.

Magnús tells his story of my visiting Hvanneyri and the fun the students had with me, especially when I taught them some folk dances. He presents me with a large, white fluffy lambskin with a thank you written in Icelandic calligraphy on the back. My Borgar-nes math teacher did the elegant calligraphy. Such a special gift with all the arduous work that went into it.

Everyone stands up. I realize I need to muster up the courage to give a little thank you speech in Icelandic, which I hope, when translated, meant this:

I want to thank Ásta, Jón, and the Borgarnes Rotary Club for a pleasant stay. I will never forget you and the year I stayed in Iceland because of the special part this has played in my life.

I'm not sure if anyone understood the words. Hopefully, they at least understood the sentiment.

The Rotarians take turns signing my new Icelandic sheepskin, which is quite heavy and sizeable. Now I know why Ásta was wondering how the gift would fit into my already full luggage.

I feel sentimental leaving my last Borgarnes Rotary meeting, knowing my stay here is ending. I reflect on all the challenging times and remind myself how these experiences were overshadowed by numerous bright, colorful rainbows.

I head home to Ásta to show her the sheepskin she already knew about. No, she says, Jón didn't tell me. I have my way of finding out about these things.

The Rotarians also gave a great big thanks and appreciation to Jón and Ásta for being such good host parents. Jón shares these well wishes with Ásta.

Two days left in Iceland. It was difficult getting to sleep again last night. I'm sure the four cups of coffee I drank yesterday didn't help. Stefania from my Borgarnes' class stops by and I show her my new lambskin gift. She gives me a silver spoon with "Iceland" engraved on it. We talk about the Borgarnes and Bifröst students and what everyone will be doing over the summer.

Later, Ásta is babysitting Anna's kids. During *kaffi*, Ásta Björk and Jón Bjarni sit close to me, and I present Ásta Björk with a sterling silver necklace and Jón Bjarni with a game of pick-up sticks. Ásta Björk tells me, The necklace is the prettiest thing I've ever owned.

It's been a pleasure to play and talk with the kids this year. Anna comes to pick them up and she says, You've filled the kids' arms with gifts!

I'm so glad to see the kids enjoying them. Anna shows off her short new haircut, which is charming and fits her personality well. I'm sure going to miss Anna and her family. She's been my stable rock in Borgarnes, always ready with a smile and a talk whenever I'm homesick.

Ásta Margrét invites me to the movie, *The Count of Monte Cristo*, with her and a friend. During intermission, I buy a Coke and a package of *Hrís* (chocolate-covered corn puffs). This could be my last time ordering a Coke in Icelandic. I wonder if I'll still think it is the best-tasting Coke in the world once I go home.

When the movie is over at eleven, it's still broad daylight. Sigga, Steinar, and Ágústa are over visiting with homemade beers in hand. They spend much of the night arguing over the name of a town I'm unfamiliar with. I occupy myself by playing on the Hi-Q pegboard, a solitaire-type game. They say their goodnights, and before Ásta goes downstairs to take a sauna, she gives me a firm hug and an Icelandic kiss. It hasn't been a terribly unpleasant year? She asks. *Nei, nei*, I reassure her.

On my last morning in Borgarnes, I complete my packing. We have blueberry *skýr* for lunch, and I take one more look around the house and backyard. Anna and Bubbi stop in, and I give Anna the handmade wooden necklace I saved for her. We're on our way as I take one last glimpse of Borgarnes. I look up the street at the steep stairway I used to climb to school, the streets I walked to Sigga's to play piano, and then I see Ásta Margrét starting out on another ring walk. I admire her kind nature, eagerness to help, and efforts to make others happy. She's become like a younger sister to me. I wave to her as she gives me a big smile.

In the backseat of the car, I sit amidst Ásta and Jón's heavy cigarette smoke, with the sunshiny weather outside, on my last trip over these stunning fjords and mountainous views. I'm going to miss the countryside dotted with sheep and Icelandic horses. We stop at the *Nesti* at Hvalfjörður. No whales are in sight during my last visit. When we arrive at Svandís and Birgir's, I learn that Glen stopped by to pick up my Luxembourg plane ticket for his friend to use. He mistakenly took my entire ticket, including my return portion to Chicago. I quickly call him to arrange for him to bring it back.

I tell Svandís I'm going for a walk, and she asks me to stop by her cousin's house to return a raincoat. I'm thankful for the assignment, as this gives a purpose to my walk. Didda and Íris are the only ones at home. We talk about my trip around Iceland. Didda tells me, I understand your Icelandic completely. Her compliment is a reward for all my months of hard work.

In the living room, the grown-ups are drinking home-brewed beer, and Ásta asks, Are you excited, love? It's too soon to try to sum up my stay. I've had challenging times as well as exciting ones. I look out the window and soak up the view of Iceland at night with my favorite navy-blue mountains framing the horizon.

On June 9, my last morning in Iceland, I'm awakened by someone coming into the TV room where I'm sleeping. When I realize it's Svandís, I give her a big hug and a smile. Her response is to plant kisses on my face and give me several strong hugs as she gives me a heartfelt, Thank you. Next, Birgir comes in and does the same. I'll sure miss them. They have been the backbone of my stay to help me survive this year. After a quick breakfast, I run to catch the bus downtown one last time.

I select a pair of hand-knit Icelandic wool "TV socks" in one of the tiny closet-sized souvenir shops downtown. These socks get their name as they are designed to keep your feet warm while watching TV. I'm delighted to recognize the woman who works in the shop. I aim to avoid any salesperson who speaks English to me since this is my last opportunity to speak Icelandic. Despite the expense, I buy three miniature Icelandic wool sheep since I know they'll make perfect gifts.

Ásta prepares what she calls "fine food" for my last meal, which turns out to be lamb chops. I help in the kitchen and peel the tiny

Icelandic potatoes one more time. Ásta makes Vigfus go to the neighborhood store to buy Coke to make it special.

I'm not missing the irony of spending my remaining precious moments in Iceland playing solitaire. I'm nervous about my departure, and since I don't care for long goodbyes, the card game helps soothe my nerves. With two cars going to the airport, I ride with Anna and Bubbi. Anna reminisces about my stay in Iceland, glossing over the strong emotions we're both feeling by telling me about the latest gossip in Borgarnes.

When we arrive at the Keflavík Airport, Anna and I head out into the windy walkway. I remember how nervous I was the first day I arrived in Iceland, how dark and foggy it was, and how I had no idea what was in store for me. Throughout the year, I've experienced many forms of ice and rainbows that have burst from hardships into friendships.

Pushing my heavy metal trunk through the airport doorway, along with my suitcase and two carry-ons, I try to be inconspicuous with the extra luggage. I'm re-exposed to English at the ticket counter when I start to speak to the airline attendant in Icelandic. She raises her eyebrows and says, Pardon me? I struggle to remember how to respond in English.

Once I've checked in my luggage, I have a few remaining minutes with my host family. As we exchange Icelandic kisses, I tell them, *Ég get ekki sagt nógu þakkir. Bara bless verður að gera* (I can't say thank you enough. Just goodbye will have to do).

This is followed by tears flowing down all our cheeks. I cross over to the other side of customs, outside onto the runway, and up the stairway onto the Icelandair flight, taking my last breath in Iceland. I'm out of Icelandic ice and rainbows for this year.

On the plane, I can't leave Iceland without humming one of my favorite tunes I picked up during the year. I will sing it to all the little children I get to know and love.

Dansi Dúkkan Mín (Dance My Doll) by Björgvin Halldórsson

Dansi, dansi dúkkan mín, dæmlauster stúlkan fín
Með voða fallegt hrokkið hár, hettan rauð og kjóllinn blár.
Svoer hún með silkiskó, sokka hvíta, einsog snjó.
Heldurðu ekki að hún sé fín,
Dansi dúkkan mín.

Dance, dance doll of mine, non-judgmental girl fine
with beautiful curly hair, hood red and dress blue.
Then she has silk shoes, socks white, like snow.
Don't you think that she is fine,
dance, dance doll of mine.

———◇———

It was no ordinary year. Over 40 years later, I realize the profound impact my stay in Iceland has had on me. It provided the foundation for my future career, avocations, and travel.

It instilled my passion for photography and I currently work as a freelance photographer. Living in Iceland spurred my interest in studying different education systems and exploring other cultures. As a result, I've participated in study programs in Czechoslovakia (now the Czech Republic) and Mexico. In 1982, I received another Rotary Scholarship during my junior year of college to attend the Australian National University in Canberra, Australia. I am indebted to the Rotary Club International for the opportunity to study

Australian politics and Aboriginal Studies at the university level. This time everything was in English, with a lovely Australian accent.

Education and international friendship became my primary career and avocation. I worked for thirty years as a researcher at the University of Wisconsin-Madison, investigating educational innovations and reforms, including educational policies for English Language Learners. I have also traveled extensively, touring every continent except Antarctica. My husband, Dan, and I have hosted over 25 foreign students in a short-term housing program. We also created a group called Village Dance House to sponsor international music groups and give concerts. I served as the photographer for the Madison World Music Festival.

Challenging as it was, learning Icelandic instilled my passion for language learning. Since my year in Iceland, I've studied Spanish, Czech, German, and Hungarian, plus a little French and Italian. My husband and I now travel yearly to Playa del Carmen, Mexico, where I continue to improve my conversational Spanish.

I have stood by my determination to not have children. This is by no means because I don't like kids. Anyone who has seen me around kids can attest to that. I made this decision before living in Iceland. However, articulating it so often to my Icelandic friends helped me to better express my reasons for taking this path. Rather than having my own children, I devote my energy and love to children already on this planet.

Ultimately, my Icelandic experience was about being an outsider trying to fit in. I went to Iceland thrilled at the prospect of experiencing a different culture, language, and way of life. While I recorded many compliments on my Icelandic, I did not become fluent in that short time. It's just that each compliment meant so much to me that I made sure to record them. I had a specific range of topics and vocabulary with which I was comfortable, and once the conversation strayed from those topics, I was pretty lost.

While I expected to learn about the people and hopefully master the language, I soon realized that to fully adopt the culture, I needed to fit in better. I wanted to experience the culture from the inside. This desire motivated me to learn the language and customs of those around me. Nevertheless, I was an outsider. Anyone who has studied or lived in another country can relate to feeling out of place. While I made great strides at fitting in, it takes a long time to fully adopt a new language and culture, which is why I have made many return visits.

SUMMER/SUMAR 2021

———— ◇ ————

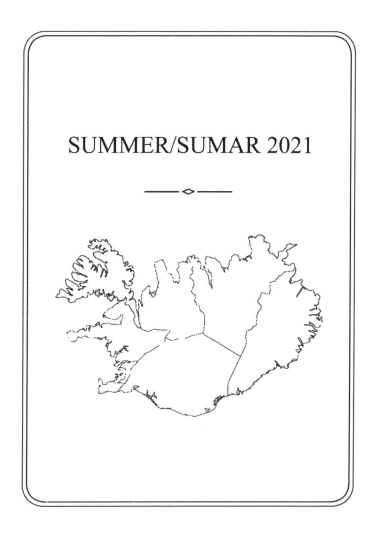

EPILOGUE

My husband, Dan, and I return to Iceland in June 2021 for my fifth visit. I want to reconnect with my host family and see both old and new sights. Iceland was one of the first countries that opened its doors to visitors after COVID-19 vaccinations became widely available. We received ours as soon as possible and planned this trip to coincide with the summer solstice. We pick up a rental car at the Keflavík airport to drive the circle route around the country. I am looking forward to visiting some of the same fjords and towns where I stopped during my cargo ship tour in 1978.

Even after all these years, I still feel overwhelming joy when I think about having lived in Iceland as an exchange student. What a powerful experience it was. Planning a trip back over forty years later, I wonder what has changed, how much Icelandic I will remember, and what it will be like to revisit my host family and old familiar places such as Borgarnes and Bifröst.

We are invited to stay with Ásta Margrét and her family for a few days before starting our road trip. After 43 years, it is predictable that I would find significant changes in my host family. During my school year in Iceland, Ásta Margrét was 14 years old, two years younger than me. She is still two years younger, but now she has been married for several decades with three grown sons and grand-children. Her grandparents, Ásta and Jón, who were my host parents, are long deceased, and a few years ago, her mother, Svandís, passed away. Her father, Birgir, has sold the house where he and Svandís lived after moving out of the apartment where I stayed with them. He now lives in a top-floor flat overlooking the ocean.

The first few days back in Iceland, we spend reminiscing about old times and talking about the family over several wonderful meals. Each day, we drive to downtown Reykjavík to look at the buildings, shops, and restaurants. We meet up with Birgir, who gives us a tour of a customs boat, like the cargo ship I took around the island. We walk through the downtown area and find a cozy café called *Teo og Kaffi* (Tea and Coffee), right next to Ingólfur Square. The surprise for me is that the town square doesn't look as prominent as before. In 1977, I thought of it as the main downtown square. With all the changes and construction, it doesn't look major anymore. We walk up a windy street to the oldest part of Reykjavík on Grjótagata Street, with its beautiful old wooden houses and lovely gardens.

We take some time to visit one of the leading regional attrac-tions, the Blue Lagoon. I'm surprised how popular the Blue Lagoon has become, as it didn't even exist when I lived in Iceland. Now they are charging more than $50 U.S. just to swim in it. Ásta Margrét tells me that she and her family do not need to go to the Blue Lagoon when they have the local Seltjarnarnes swimming pool just a few minutes away. The local pool is also heated by the hot springs and costs $8 U.S. a visit, or even less with an annual family pass.

Close to the Blue Lagoon is the Fagradalsfjall volcano that has recently erupted. Using the plume of smoke in the sky to guide us, we drive toward the southwest corner of the peninsula. We set out on foot and come over a slight rise to see the bright, orange, boiling lava heading our way. A large crowd of people is oohing and ahhing at the spectacular sight. We try to take a step closer but are pushed back by a massive gust of heat. Some curious tourists attempt to touch the black lava, thinking it had cooled, and they shriek in pain as their fingers burn. On our way back to Reykjavík through the back roads, we visit several picturesque, untouched waterfalls, old rural churches, and hot pools of bubbling sulfur water.

After spending a few days with Ásta Margrét and her family, we begin our circle tour around the island. Our first stop is Borgarnes, where I spent the initial part of my school year. This also means we start our circle tour clockwise on the map, the same direction as my boat trip in 1978. In Borgarnes, we check into a guesthouse and meet up with Anna, the daughter-in-law of my host parents, Ásta and Jón.

Anna surprises us with a visit to the house where I lived with my host parents, now home to an American artist. The new owner gives us a full tour, complete with a fantastic view out the huge picture windows in the living room, devoid of the heavy curtains I remember. We admire her large, colorful fantasy paintings displayed around the house and in the lower-level art studio. She has mastered Icelandic, so we speak in Icelandic together while Anna and I reminisce about what the house looked like when I lived there. I point to the pantry where we stored the 18 varieties of cookies that Ásta and I made together for Christmas in 1977.

Anna hosts a big dinner party for us, complete with champagne, smoked mutton, and salmon. We both have a good laugh as Anna points to the obligatory canned green peas. Her husband Bubbi joins us as well as their two kids and grandkids. A special surprise guest is Árni, Svandís and Bubbi's younger brother, who was an exchange student in Illinois while I stayed with his parents in Borgarnes. I met Árni when I was 16, after he arrived in the United States and came to visit me in Green Bay shortly before I left for Iceland. We wrote to each other a few times that year, but I haven't seen him again until this night. He was always out of the country on my previous visits to

Iceland. It's delightful to reminisce about his parents and compare notes about our experiences as exchange students.

In the morning, we drive with Anna and her daughter, Ásta Björk, out to the tip of the Snæfellsnes Peninsula. Along the way, they point out the farmhouse where the mother and daughter helped remove the big wad of chewing gum from my hair back in 1977. Unlike so many years ago, we do not climb the glacier this time. Although now, I would know to be better prepared. Anna and Ásta Björk's enthusiasm for hiking matches the Icelandic trait of loving to explore the countryside. We set out on several trails, first to a volcanic crater and then across cliffs overlooking the ocean. The weather is spectacular, with rare and beautiful views of the glacier.

As we're hiking, Ásta Björk and I have fun remembering the days when she and her younger brother would come over to visit and I would play with them. Ásta Björk is now married with two kids and lives just a few houses away from her grandparents' house (Ásta and Jón's) where I stayed.

We stop in the town of Hellnar on the peninsula and walk down the hill to Fjöruhúsið Café, overlooking the water. Anna tries to speak with the waitress in Icelandic. The waitress doesn't understand her and I discover she is Czech. Since I've studied the language, I order for us in Czech. This is new to encounter immigrants living and working in Iceland. The fish soup we order is $23 a bowl, which reminds me of how expensive the country can be. The redeeming value is that the soup is delicious.

We take a few more hikes around the peninsula and then stop at the small town of Grundarfjörður, famous for its fish. While ordering our meal at the Bjargarsteinn Mathús Restaurant, Ásta Björk points out the Icelandic actor Björn Hlynur Haraldsson. He played a policeman from Reykjavík in the Netflix TV series Ófært (Trapped). Anna encourages me to talk to him, saying he would be pleased as Icelanders don't make a big deal about movie stars or celebrities. With the country's current population of 350,000, famous actors, politicians, and celebrities are not out of the ordinary. Even if Icelandic popstar Björk walked into a café, she wouldn't cause a stir.

The next day, we make an excursion to the east of Borgarnes with Anna, Ásta Björk, and Jón Bjarni's wife, Anna, and her kids. Our first stop is the Víðgelmir lava chute, a cave formed by lava that cut through an opening in the earth and left behind a long, deep cave. Nearby, we drive up into the hills to view a waterfall and take in the natural hot pools at Húsafell Canyon Baths.

We are amazed by the Barnafossar waterfalls (Children's Falls), which we had seen before but are even more dazzled by this time. Barnafossar is a series of rapids bursting out of the surrounding lava plains. The name comes from a legend about two brothers who fell into the river after slipping on a bridge. As a result, the mother had the bridge destroyed and cast a spell on the waterfall, claiming no one would ever be able to cross it and survive.

Our last stop is Húsafell, a crossroads with a small church and artist workshop. At the homestead, we are treated to Ásta Björk's homemade Icelandic *pönnukökur* (pancakes). Inside the church, known for its acoustics, Anna and Ásta Björk sing an Icelandic song for us, and I follow with a Czech tune. On our way back to Borgarnes, we stop for a tribe of goats crossing the road, a rare find and an excellent photo opp.

Just before leaving Borgarnes, we stop at one of the newer, larger grocery stores on the outskirts of town, where I purchase a Prince Polo chocolate bar for old-time's sake. It still has that same familiar chocolate wafery flavor, bringing back memories. This time, I buy a Coke to go along with it, rather than the chocolate milk we used to buy during class breaks in Borgarnes. I conclude that Coke still does taste better in Iceland.

Our next destination is Bifröst, where I lived at the boarding school for four months. Currently, it serves as a university and is used as a hotel in the summer. The drive from Borgarnes to Bifröst feels much shorter, probably because of improved road conditions and my improved sense of well-being compared to those long, lonely drives 43 years ago. I am flying high with emotions as we spend a few hours walking through the school, looking at the classrooms, cafeteria, common study areas, library, and dormitory. Everything looks a little out of proportion. My dorm room doesn't seem to be in the exact location I remember, and the original building looks smaller and dated. Since Bifröst has been converted into a university, it has new additions with an expanded library, theater, and dormitories. I see that the cafeteria has remained the same. I reminisce about the days long past that I spent here.

When we walk through the basement hallway where former class photos are posted on the wall. I see all my classmates in the 1977-78 school year photos. In the bottom right corner is a small black and white photo of the only student without an Icelandic name, Paula White, proudly wearing an Icelandic hand-knit wool sweater. The outsider trying to fit in.

As we intentionally travel to Iceland to be here during the summer solstice, we arrive in Akureyri on the longest day of the year. It took eight hours to drive to Akureyri from Bifröst in 1978. Now that the roads have improved, the driving time is reduced to three hours. I am delighted to return to Akureyri and revisit the striking downtown church, the harbor, the botanic garden, and the swimming pool. The city has grown considerably since my last visit forty-three years ago, with a larger population and more shops and cafes. Akureyri is located just 62 miles below the artic circle. The sun does set on the longest day, only it never gets completely dark.

When we order a plate of fish and chips from an outdoor cart, I am surprised to learn that the cart's operator is from Poland. Meeting another European immigrant demonstrates the trend in Iceland of hiring more immigrants to work in service-related jobs. The vendor has lived in Akureyri for seven years but doesn't speak much Icelandic. He communicates with customers in English. He explains how much he loves living in here and how his income is significantly higher than it would be back in Poland.

From Akureyri, we visit a few port towns I had visited on my cargo ship ring tour of Iceland in 1978. Now in 2021, we drive to Siglufjörður, in the far north, where episodes of *Ófærð* (Trapped) were filmed. The actor we met earlier was in this TV series. We visit the Herring Era Museum, which specializes in the history of herring fisheries in Iceland and learn the significant role herring once played in Iceland's economy.

Revisiting the town of Husavík, I recognize the hillside and harbor. The town has grown with many more houses, shops, and whale-watching excursions. This is the town where the 2020 movie *Eurovision Song Contest, The Story of Fire Saga* was set. The film introduced the song *"Husavík My Hometown."* The movie is popular among Icelanders, and the song was nominated for an Oscar.

We climb a hillside in Husavík that's covered in purple lupines. I am surprised to see so many of the colorful flowers throughout our drive. While I remember seeing them in Akureyri on my spring trip in 1978, they weren't this widespread. The flower has caused a division among Icelanders. Supporters praise the virtues of the lupines as a soil conservation tool. Opponents complain that lupines are an introduced plant that disrupts the traditional landscape.

Next, we spend three days in the Lake Mývatn area, where we hike and visit locations used in the filming of the Game of Thrones series. We swim in the Mývatn Nature Baths and enjoy the luxurious hot water even though the weather is extremely windy and just 50 degrees Fahrenheit in mid-summer. We meet a couple from Switzerland who just traveled from Borgafjörður Eystri, where they saw hundreds of puffins. It is out of our way, but we decide to make the drive the next day because we cannot resist the opportunity to see puffins.

While the ring road through the east fjords and the south is now fully paved, it is an elevated, often winding, narrow road with no shoulders or guard rails. Though wide enough for two cars to pass, it feels like our car could easily get pushed off down the embankment. The section of the road out to Borgafjörður Eystri is especially hair-raising, with a slow long switchback climb over a mountain and down into the fjord. We are rewarded for our strain as we approach the colony of puffins. The birds don't seem to mind the twenty or so tourists standing among them on the observation decks. On the crown of the hill, the puffins are perched in dug-out holes. We are delighted to spend several hours observing the cute and, at times, humorous puffins as they peek out of their burrows, sun themselves, and fly around in search of food.

Continuing the circle route, we visit Höfn, the town I missed when circling the island by ship in 1978 due to the stormy weather. When we check into the guesthouse in Höfn, we discover that the receptionist is also Polish. She invites us to a town dance featuring an Icelandic band playing American jazz that evening. Meanwhile, on the back porch of the guesthouse, we meet an Icelandic couple, share some wine, and learn that we have a shared interest in photography. We quickly become Facebook friends and discover that we already have a mutual friend, Anna, the wife of Anna and Bubbi's son, Jón Bjarni. Once again, I am reminded of the country's sparse population, with very few degrees of separation between anyone we meet.

We visit Diamond Beach and the Jökulsárlón lagoon, which sits at the base of the Breiðamerkurjökull Glacier. The lagoon is filled with icebergs that have split off from the glacier. This stop is one of the most spectacular sights I've seen along the ring road. As the icebergs drift out to the ocean, some get stuck in the black sand, giving the impression that they are large diamonds, hence the name "Diamond Beach. "A famous car chase across the frozen lagoon was featured in the 2002 James Bond film "*Die Another Day.* "

The next stop is the town of Vík on the south coast. We stay at a guest house overlooking a beautiful red church on the hillside. This is the town where the supernatural thriller "*Katla*" was filmed, another Icelandic TV series that we enjoy. The thriller is about changelings born under the Katla volcano that sits above the town. As we watch one of the episodes in the guesthouse, we see the town church and the famous offshore rocks, both out our windows and in the *Katla* episode on our laptop. We walk out on the sand, close to the rocks, where we admire the photogenic scene of a line of horseback riders as they cast shadows on the black beach.

As we approach Þórsmörk, I'm tempted to turn in and make up for the weather fiasco in 1978. I remember how I was spared one fog-free moment in the magical water wonderland. However, our ring trip is nearing an end, so we must postpone Þórsmörk for now.

We travel on to Hveragerði, the town famous for its greenhouses which I visited on my first trip to Iceland. The greenhouses provide a continuous supply of vegetables throughout most of the year. We take some pleasant walks in the hills above the town, where we see geothermal steam vents dotting the landscape. Many sports fans at a local pub are watching the Euro 2020 football (soccer) tournament which was delayed due to the pandemic. We enjoy watching the tournament with the locals. I don't know much about soccer, but I'm pleased to be able to translate the Icelandic narration for my husband.

We finish the circle tour with the same stops I made on a day tour in 1978. We visit the Great Geysir, which I'm reminded is the source of the word "geyser." Although no longer active, other spouting geysers and bubbling vents are in the same field. Not far to the north is the spectacular Gullfoss or "Golden Falls." The Hvítá river travels from the Langjökull glacier, then falls over 100 feet in two separate drops. Our last stop is Þingvellir National Park, the original home of the Alþing, Iceland's parliament. The current parliament sits in Reykjavík. The Alþing is the oldest continuously functioning parliament in the world. Another highlight of the vast national park is our walk through the rift valley along the crest of the Mid-Atlantic Ridge, the boundary between the North American and Eurasian tectonic plates.

Our last two nights are spent with Ásta Margrét and her family in Reykjavík. We return downtown to the shops and our favorite café. A long pedestrian street leading up to the Hallgrímskirkja Church is painted in rainbow stripes, confirming that Iceland is indeed a land of ice and rainbows.

While driving the circle route, I noticed significant changes since my school year here over 40 years ago. The roads are in much better shape. Not only rural roads but some roads through towns were gravel back in the 1970s. Currently, several bridges cross the fjords, and the entire ring road around the country is paved. Perhaps this accessibility, together with other development, is one of the reasons the Icelandic landscape is used as a filming location for many popular TV series and movies. Even though it wasn't on our itinerary, we found five filming locations on our drive.

Many more trees dot the landscape since reforestation efforts have been underway to rebuild some of the lost forests. The forests were lost centuries ago due to wood harvesting for housing and fuel. New, established wooded areas and the introduction of lupines have noticeably changed the look and feel of parts of the country.

We do not need to use any cash. Every shop, grocery store, restaurant, and even small outside food and merchandise stalls accept credit cards.

The young, primarily Polish, Eastern European labor force working in shops, restaurants, and hotels is easily noticed. According to a Wikipedia entry, Polish immigrants in Iceland currently number over 20,000, or five percent of the population.

Iceland has become a popular destination with many more tourist services and tourists. Icelanders are more engaged in foreign travel, and foreigners are more prevalent, accepted, and appreciated in Iceland than ever before.

Even with these changes, Iceland is still recognizable as the country I learned to love over forty years ago. The landscape is broadly the same, with lava everywhere but now dotted with golf courses and skateboard courts right next to the lava fields. By circling the circumference of the country, we've seen something outstanding each day: the fjords, the waterfalls, the Icelandic horses, the puffins, the swans, and the glaciers. This most recent trip reminds me how lucky I was to take a cargo ship through so many fjords and stop at so many ports. The tall sloping hillsides head straight into the coast, forming a narrow body of water from the ocean into the end of the inlet. I remember the snow drizzling down the sides of the narrow inlets, like icing on a cake, with the glaciers melting into the mountainsides like tongues.

It is rewarding to hear compliments about my spoken Icelandic, even more than 40 years later, with hardly any opportunity to practice. I guess my vigorous efforts as a 16-year-old paid off. It's still a wonder to me that I had so much enthusiasm at that young age to speak only Icelandic.

When I confront the medic who gives my husband a COVID test, I am satisfied with my recall of Icelandic. I hear my husband scream when the swab is sent way up his nose, making it unnecessarily painful. I surprise myself when I yell at the medic in Icelandic, *Þú mátt ekki gera það* (You mustn't do that)! After all these years, I have found a valuable opportunity to express myself in Icelandic.

A woman from Maryland whom we meet at our guesthouse in Hveragerði tells us that after her second day in Iceland, she feels she could live in Iceland forever as she's fallen in love with the countryside. Her comment makes me think how much easier it is to fall in love with Iceland if visiting during the peak of the summer when everything is lovely and green, without experiencing the long, cold, dark winters. Over forty years later, I still love the language, the landscapes, the culture, and the people, but not the weather or the isolation. Thank you, Iceland, my host country. Thank you, my lovely host family. I hope to return soon. For now, a kiss on the lips, *bless*, *bless*.

Who's Who and How They Got Their Names

Icelandic Naming Conventions

Icelanders have no surnames. Icelandic last names are configured as the first name of the father followed by an "s" and then -son ("son") or -dóttir (daughter). I initially found this confusing, so here is an example from my host family.

Jón Björnsson (father)

Svandís Jónsdóttir (daughter to Jón)

Björn Jónsson (son to Jón)

Ásta Björk Björnsdóttir (daughter to Björn and granddaughter to Jón)

Jón Bjarni Björnsson (son to Björn and grandson to Jón)

A man and a woman get married. The man's name is *Jón Björnsson* and the woman's name is *Ásta Sigurðsdóttir*. When they marry, they both keep their names just as they are. When Ásta and Jón have a baby girl, they name her Svandís, and her last name becomes Jónsdóttir because her father's first name is Jón. A few years later, they have a baby boy and name him Björn. His last name becomes Jónsson, as he is the son of Jón. The reason for the difference in the last name is their gender. The ending "son" is for males and "dóttir" for females. Women do not take their husband's last name when they get married (because they don't become the "son" of their husband's father). However, just as typical in most of the world, the wife's name is lost to the next generation.

In the above example, if Björn Jónsson were to have a son and name him Jón, the child's name would be Jón Björnsson, just like his grandfather. It is common across generations for the male lineage to have this flip-flopping pattern of first-name-last-name switching. This also means that a family member will generally have a different last name from their parents and siblings of another gender.

An exception would be successive generations of sons named after their father and grandfather. (Consider generations of Jón Jónsson).

Current laws in Iceland now allow for some gender neutrality. First names have been traditionally and legally assigned by gender. For example, parents can't name their daughter "Björn." Iceland has a finite list of legal first names with a separate list for males and females. A few names are on both lists. Any new name that reflects gender neutrality needs approval from the Icelandic Naming Committee. Petitions for name changes can only come from individuals who reject the gender categories of male and female. These individuals are also allowed to adopt a gender-neutral suffix of "bur" or "barn" (meaning "child"). Yet they still must add this suffix to their father's given name.

My Extended Icelandic Family

My host parents:
Jón Björnsson and Ásta Sigurðsdóttir, residing in Borgarnes
Their children:
Svandís Jónsdóttir married Birgir Vigfusson, residing in Seltjarnarnes near Reykjavík
> Their Children: Ásta Margrét, Vigfus, Birgir Jón, Linda Björg

Björn (Bubbi) Jónsson married Anna Ólafsdóttir, residing in Borgarnes
> Their Children: Ásta Björk, Jón Bjarni

Árni (Addi) Jónsson, from Borgarnes, in 1977-78, lived in Illinois as a Rotary exchange student

My Wisconsin Family

Betty White, mom
Keith White, dad
Sayward White, sister
Starker White, brother
Robin White, sister
Dana White, sister

Glossary of Icelandic Terms and Locations

- Afskaplega gott – extremely good.
- Akranes – a port town and municipality on the west coast of Iceland.
- Akureyri – a city nicknamed the "Capital of North Iceland" at the base of Eyjafjörður Fjord in northern Iceland.
- Alþing – is the national parliament of Iceland. It is the oldest legislature in the world that still exists. It was founded in 930 at Þingavellir, 45 kilometers east of Iceland's capital, Reykjavík.
- Alveg frábært – absolutely great.
- Að bjóða heilsu – to bid health.
- Bandarikyunum – the United States.
- Bifröst – a small settlement in western Iceland and the site of the Bifröst Junior College and boarding school.
- Bless bless – good-bye.
- Blóðmör – blood pudding.
- Bolladagur – bun day.
- Borgarnes – a town located on a peninsula at the shore of Borgarfjörður.
- Brennivín – burning wine, a strong Icelandic liquor distilled from fermented grain mash and flavored with caraway.
- Ég veit ekki – I don't know.
- Ekkert að þakka – you're welcome.
- Ekkert gott að segja – nothing good to say.
- Elskan mín – my dear or my darling.
- Elsku Pála mín, komdu að borða – my dear Paula, come to eat.
- Er allt í lagi – are you all right?
- Erfitt – difficult.
- Eyja – island.

- Fjörður – fjord.

- Fyrirgevðu – excuse me.

- Gaman – fun.

- Gamal dans – old dance.

- Geysir – a geyser in western Iceland from which all geysers get their name.

- Goða nott – good night.

- Goðan daginn – good day.

- Grábrók – a crater formed by a fissure eruption approximately three thousand years ago.

- Grænar baunir – green peas, the popular canned vegetable served at nearly every meal in Iceland.

- Gullfoss – Golden Falls, one of Iceland's most iconic waterfalls.

- Fint strákur – nice boy.

- Hangikjöt – smoked mutton.

- Harðfiskur – dried fish.

- Heimabakað – homemade.

- Heimaey – Home Island, the largest and only inhabited island of the Westmann Islands archipelago.

- Heyrðu elskan – hey dear.

- Hvalfjörður – Whale Fjord, a deep fjord that reaches far inland just north of Reykjavík.

- Hveragerði – known as the greenhouse and hot spring town.

- Hæ – hi.

- Já – yes.

- Jæja – well.

- Jökull – glacier.

- Kaffi – coffee, or the afternoon snack when coffee, tea, or other beverages are served with cakes and sweets.

- Keflavík – a town close to Reykjavík where the international airport is located.
- Kópavogar – a town just south of Reykjavík.
- Krónur – plural form of *króna,* the Icelandic currency.
- Laxveiði – salmon fishing.
- Lifrapylsa – liver sausage.
- Mikið gaman – very fun.
- Nei – no.
- Paskahret – a special word meaning bad weather during Easter time.
- Reykjavík – Iceland's capital city.
- Rúgbrauð – dark rye bread.
- Seltjarnarnes – a town on the peninsula close to Reykjavík.
- Skýr – an Icelandic cultured dairy product. It has the consistency of Greek yogurt but a milder flavor and has been a part of Icelandic cuisine for centuries.
- Skál – cheers.
- Slátur – slaughter, a type of Icelandic haggis made from sheep's innards.
- Snæfellsnes Glacier – a 700,000-year-old glacier-capped volcano in western Iceland.
- Surtsey – the youngest island of the Westmann Islands archipelago, formed in 1963.
- Svið – boiled sheep's head, a traditional Icelandic dish that involves cutting the sheep's head in half and boiling it in water with the brain removed.
- Takk – thanks.
- Úti – out, used to refer to "outside" the country.
- Útivist – outside time or outside activities.
- Útlandingur – foreigner.

- Vestmannaeyjar – the Westman Islands, an archipelago off Iceland's south coast, formed by underwater volcanic eruptions.

- Það er nefnilega það – that is namely that.

- Þakka þér fyrir – thank you.

- Þingvellir – a national park and site of Iceland's parliament from the 10th to the 18th centuries.

- Þórsmörk – a valley in the southern highlands of Iceland.

*Note on Icelandic pronunciation: the letters ð (eth) and þ (thorn) represent the English "th" sound, voiced and unvoiced, respectively.

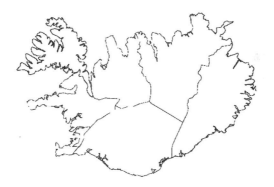

Icelandic Recipes

Brauðsúpa (Bread Soup)

My host mother made bread soup frequently. At first, I found the taste strange and was surprised to learn that it was made with rye bread. Over time, it became a favorite of mine and she would make it especially for me. The soup is best served warm with a dollop of fresh whipped cream.

Ingredients

4 slices light rye bread, chopped (5 cups)
3 slices whole/dark rye bread, chopped (3 cups)
½ cup lingonberry or sour cherry jam
¼ cup sugar, or more to taste
½ cup raisins
water, as needed

Directions

1. Add the cubed bread to a pot and cover with water.
2. Stir in the jam and bring to a simmer. Puree with an immersion blender until smooth.
3. Add raisins and sugar to taste. Continue simmering until the bread thickens, about 10 minutes. Taste and add more water or sugar if necessary.
4. Serve hot or chilled, garnished with more raisins. Add a dollop of whipped cream.

Lambasúpa (Lamb Soup)

Ingredients

2 tablespoons olive oil
1 teaspoon finely chopped garlic
1 medium chopped onion
½ teaspoon dried thyme
½ teaspoon dried oregano
½ chopped cabbage
4 carrots cut into ½-inch slices
½ diced rutabaga
1 cup cauliflower florets
4 potatoes sliced into ½-inch cubes
½ cup brown rice
4 ½ cups water
3 ½ lbs. lamb chops cubed

Directions

1. Add olive oil to a large pot set on medium heat.
2. Add garlic and sauté for one-to-two minutes.
3. Add lamb cubes and sear on all sides until browned.
4. Add chopped onion and fry for one minute or until onion is softened on the edges but not all the way through.
5. Add water and brown rice. Increase heat to high and bring to a boil for five minutes.
6. Reduce heat to medium and stir in thyme and oregano.
7. Cover and continue cooking for 40 minutes.
8. Add cauliflower, cabbage, carrots, rutabaga, and potatoes.
9. Cover and cook for 20 minutes.

Laxasúpa (Salmon Soup)

Ingredients

2 lbs. salmon steaks
4 cups water
½ cup heavy cream
½ cup sherry
2 bay leaves
2 carrots, chopped small
1 small onion, chopped small
Stems from a bunch of parsley, chopped
Stems from a bunch of dill, chopped
Salt and pepper to taste
16 prunes, stoned and cut into 4 pieces
½ cup raisins
1 tablespoon butter
1 tablespoon flour
Juice of half a lemon
1 tablespoon sugar

Directions

1. Bring the water to a boil in a pan with bay leaves, carrots, onion, parsley, dill, and salt and pepper to taste. Add sherry.
2. Add the salmon and simmer at low heat until the fish is cooked through and just beginning to come off the bones.
3. Strain all but ½ cup of the stock into a clean pan. Add prunes and raisins to the stock and bring to a boil.
4. Cut the softened butter into the flour and whisk into the prune and raisin stock to thicken it. Add heavy cream.
5. Combine all the contents of the fish pan into the prune pot.
6. Simmer for 5 to 8 minutes. Add lemon juice and sugar and season to taste.

Humar/Rækju Salat (Lobster/Shrimp Salad)

Ingredients

1 ½ pounds cooked lobster meat or shrimp, chopped
1 shallot, minced
½ lemon, juiced
1 tablespoon tarragon, minced
½ cup mayonnaise
1 tablespoon whole grain mustard
1 tablespoon capers
Salt to taste

Directions

1. Mix mayonnaise, lemon juice, and mustard in a medium bowl.
2. Mince the shallot and tarragon well. Add to mayonnaise mixture.
3. Add chopped lobster meat or shrimp. Add capers.
4. Stir gently, but completely. Add salt to taste.
5. Refrigerate 30 minutes before serving.

The salad may be garnished with sliced, hard-boiled eggs.

Hrísgrjónabúðingur (Rice Pudding)

Ingredients

1 cup long grain brown rice
1 cup water
½ teaspoon salt
3 cups milk
Plus an additional 1 cup hot milk
1 teaspoon sugar
1 teaspoon cinnamon
Raisins

Directions

1. Wash the rice and place in a large saucepan along with the water and salt.
2. Allow the rice to simmer for 20 minutes, covered.
3. Pour the first 3 cups of milk into the saucepan. Simmer for 40 minutes on low heat, covered.
4. Add two handfuls of raisins and cook for 2 minutes.
5. Add 1 cup hot milk. Simmer for 5 minutes.
6. Mix together 1 teaspoon sugar and 1 teaspoon cinnamon and serve in a separate bowl as topping.

Kleinur (Twisted Donuts)

Ingredients

4 eggs
1 cup sugar
1 cup milk
½ cup sour cream
1 teaspoon baking soda
1 teaspoon ground cardamom
1 ½ teaspoons salt
About 9 cups flour (plus more for rolling)
½ to 1-gallon canola oil for frying, depending on size of fryer

Directions

1. Beat eggs well. Mix the baking soda into the sour cream, then add sugar, milk, cardamom, and salt.
2. Add flour. To mix in the last cups of flour, put dough on counter and mix with hands. Divide dough into five equal parts. Shape each into a large pancake about one inch thick. Place in plastic bags and chill until ready to use.
3. Roll dough ¼-inch thick on floured bread board. Cut into 3 x 1 ½-inch strips. Slit the centers and pull one end through the slit.
4. Fry like doughnuts. Heat oil to 350°F. Working in batches of 8-12 kleinur (depending on the size of your pot or deep fryer), place the twisted pieces of dough in the hot oil. Let cook for a few minutes until golden on one side. Flip, and allow the other side to cook.
5. Remove with tongs or a skimmer. Set the kleinur on paper towels to cool.

Pönnukökur (Icelandic Pancakes)

Ingredients

8 eggs
3 cups flour
1 teaspoon baking powder
½ teaspoon baking soda
1 teaspoon salt
1 teaspoon vanilla
½ cup melted butter
4 cups milk
1 cup sour cream

Directions

1. Mix eggs, butter, vanilla, milk, and sour cream in a bowl.
2. Combine flour, baking powder, baking soda, and salt in a separate bowl.
3. Stir dry ingredients into wet, combining well but do not over-mix.
4. Pour batter and spread thinly onto a hot, greased pan. Make one pancake at a time.
5. Makes 30-40 pancakes. This is a traditional Icelandic dish, with a wonderful texture and taste. They are tasty served warm or cool. Fill each *pönnukökur* with brown sugar or jam and roll up.

Rúgbrauð (Icelandic Rye Bread)

Ingredients

4 ½ cups medium rye flour
2 teaspoons salt
1 tablespoon baking powder
¾ teaspoon baking soda
2 cups buttermilk
½ cup honey
½ cup molasses

Directions

1. Preheat the oven to 325°F with a rack in the center position.
2. In a large bowl, whisk together the flour, salt, baking powder, and baking soda.
3. In a separate bowl, whisk together the buttermilk, honey, and molasses.
4. Pour the wet ingredients into the dry ingredients, stirring to combine.
5. Transfer the batter to a lightly greased 9" Pullman loaf pan and smooth the top. Lightly grease the lid and place on the pan.
6. Bake the bread for 2 hours. Turn off the oven and remove the lid from the pan. Leave the loaf in the turned-off oven for another 15 minutes. Then remove from the oven and turn out of the pan onto a cooling rack.
7. Cool completely before slicing thinly and serving with butter or your favorite savory toppings. Pickled herring and smoked salmon are traditional, but cheese (anything from salty aged to soft mild) is also recommended.
8. Store leftover bread tightly wrapped at room temperature for several days. Freeze for longer storage.

Skúffukaka (Icelandic Chocolate Cake)

Ingredients

2 cups flour
½ cup butter, softened
½ cup cocoa powder
1 ½ cup sugar
1 teaspoon baking soda
1 cup milk
1 teaspoon baking powder
2 eggs
1 teaspoon salt

Directions

1. Preheat oven to 350°F and lightly grease a 13x9 inch pan.
2. In a bowl, combine the dry ingredients: flour, cocoa, baking soda, baking powder, and salt.
3. In a large mixing bowl, cream sugar and butter until light and airy. Add eggs one at a time, mixing well after each addition. Add milk and mix well.
4. Add dry ingredients to the mixing bowl and mix well.
5. Transfer to a baking pan and bake for 25-30 minutes or until a toothpick inserted in the middle comes out clean.
6. Frost when the cake has cooled completely.

Frosting

2 cups powdered sugar
2 tablespoons melted butter
2 tablespoons cocoa powder
2 tablespoons hot water

Whisk 2 cups powdered sugar with 2 tablespoons cocoa powder. Blend in melted butter. Mix in hot water gradually, as needed. Let cool and spread on the cake.

Appelsínumarmelaði (Orange Marmalade)

This is not a traditional Icelandic recipe, but it's something special my host mother made that I thought was delicious.

Ingredients

3 lbs. oranges (6 to 12 oranges, depending on the size)
2 lemons
6 to 8 cups water
5 to 6 cups sugar (or more to taste)

Directions

1. Scrub fruit clean. Slice the top and bottom of each orange and lemon and discard. Slice fruit into thin rounds and cut into half-moon shapes. Discard seeds.
2. Place fruit and any accumulated fruit juice in a large pot. Add 6 to 8 cups of water, depending on the quantity of fruit.
3. Bring to a boil, then reduce heat to low and simmer for 30 minutes until the rind is just tender.
4. Add the sugar to the fruit mixture and cook on low heat until the sugar is dissolved.
5. Cover and stand overnight at room temperature.
6. Bring mixture back to a boil. Reduce to low heat, stir occasionally, and skim off any surface foam. Simmer up to 2 hours.
7. Bring to a rapid boil until it becomes a jelly-like consistency. To test, place a spoonful of jam on a saucer and set aside in the fridge for 5 minutes. It should gel. Allow the jam to cool a little (the fruit will float to the top if the jam is too hot) before bottling in sterilized jars. Store for up to 3 months.

What Makes Iceland Different (1977-78)

This list of traits, habits, customs, and facts is based on my school year in Iceland from 1977-78. These were observations I made from my own experiences and were not necessarily universal. Many have, or may have, changed since that time.

Icelandic Food and Drink

- Drinking coffee is a national pastime. Icelanders are avid coffee drinkers, and any good visit involves at least one cup.
- *Kaffi* is an early afternoon time to drink a beverage such as coffee, tea, or milk with something sweet like cake, cookies, or pastries.
- Instead of spooning sugar into the coffee, those who take sugar, place a sugar cube between the top and lower front teeth and then sip the coffee through the sugar cube.
- Ice cream is cut out of a box into slices instead of using a scoop.
- Breakfast cereal is called "cornflakes," using the English word, regardless of the brand or type of cereal.
- Icelanders love strongly flavored licorice candy.
- The Icelandic cultured dairy product *skýr*, is popular anytime, as a snack or for breakfast, lunch, and/or dinner.
- Everything imaginable is spread on bread, such as lamb, sardines, herring, vegetables, fruit salad, shrimp salad, and lobster salad.
- Just about everything is eaten with a knife and fork instead of by hand, including slices of bread, sandwiches, and pizza.
- Because of the clear Icelandic spring waters, it is believed that Coke tastes better in Iceland than anywhere else in the world.
- Drinking hard liquor, including *brennivín* (firewater) was common since beer was outlawed at the time.
- When standing up to leave the dinner table, the custom is to say, "thank you" in Icelandic while the others respond, "thanks, the same to you."

- Tap water is heated by the hot springs and comes out of the tap very hot, nearly boiling.

Icelandic Weather

- Whether it's winter or summer, there's not much temperature difference. The average summer temperature is 60 degrees Fahrenheit, and the average winter temperature is 40 degrees Fahrenheit. It's the wind chill that's brutal.

- Many Icelanders are great trekkers with a high tolerance for the cold and wind.

- Outdoor swimming pools are heated by hot springs and are open year-round.

- Due to Iceland's unique weather conditions, it's the only country in the world with no mosquitoes.

- Iceland has long stretches of darkness in the winter and long stretches of daylight in the summer.

The Icelandic Language

- Two letters in the Icelandic alphabet, ð (eth) and þ (thorn), represent the English "th' sound, voiced and unvoiced, respectively.

- *Innsog* is a typical Icelandic style of speaking while inhaling and is used to emphasize agreement and to encourage whomever you're speaking with, to continue talking. This technique is commonly used with the words *já* (yes), *nei* (no) which are repeated several times in a row, and *jæja* (well).

- Language planners invent Icelandic words for new high-tech and pop-culture terms to save the Icelandic language from extinction.

- When Icelanders speak about the United States, they refer to it as "*úti*" (out), and they do the same when referring to Europe and all other countries.

- Icelandic has been ranked as one of the hardest languages for English speakers to learn because of its archaic vocabulary and complex grammar.

- Icelandic has a reputation for lengthy words. *Vaðlaheiðarveg-avinnuverkfærageymsluskúrautidyralyklakippuhringur* is one of the longest. It means "key ring of the key chain of the outer door to the storage tool shed of the road workers on the Vaðlaheiði."

Icelandic Customs and Practices

- It was customary to kiss on the lips when greeting friends or family of any gender.

- Book-giving is a tradition for holidays such as Christmas and birthdays. The Icelandic population has nearly 100 percent literacy.

- Icelanders love to share stories and beliefs about elves and gnomes.

- Just about everyone in Iceland knows how to knit since they're taught in school. Icelandic hand-knit wool sweaters are worn by Icelanders and tourists alike.

- Icelanders are often stoic on the outside and soft on the inside. From my experience, in recent years, this stoicism has relaxed significantly.

- Iceland is expensive. Expect to pay much more for everything.

- No TV programs were offered on Thursday evenings so Icelanders could attend social events. This rule is no longer practiced.

- TV programs were presented without commercial breaks. All commercials were shown between programs.

- It is customary for friends and family to tell each other "thanks for the last time" (*takk fyrir síðast)* the next time they see each other, and "thanks for the last year" (*takk fyrir síðast ar)* on New Year's Eve.

- Because there are no surnames, the phone book lists everyone alphabetically by first name, with one phone book for the entire country. If more than one person shares the same name, the profession is listed following the name.

- Iceland has one of the highest rates of childbirth outside marriage. It is common for women to later marry the father of their child.

- Cigarette smoking was widespread in Iceland in 1977-78, among teenagers and adults alike.

- Iceland doesn't have a Santa Claus who brings Christmas presents. Instead, Iceland has a Christmas Witch, Grýla, who punishes naughty children. Grýla is said to have 13 sons, the Yule Lads, who live in the mountains and whose jobs are to steal food and scare children who misbehave.

REFERENCES

Becker, Linda, "What's In A Name? Nonbinary People In Iceland Finding Their Voice." The Reykjavík Grapevine, May 17, 2021, grapevine.is/news/2021/05/17/whats-in-a-name-nonbinary-people-in-iceland-finding-their-voice/

Boetig, Donna Elizabeth, "Out of the Ashes." An Interview with Frank McCourt in Writer's Digest, February 1999, pp. 18-21.

Glacken, Brendan, "The Awful Icelandic Language." Iceland Review, 1973, pp. 46-52.

Laxdæla Saga, translated by Magnus Magnusson and Hermann Palsson, New York; Penguin, 1969.

Outline Map of Iceland with Regions, Vemaps 2022, vemaps.com/iceland/is-02

Schneider, Caitlin, "11 Delightful Icelandic Words and Phrases," Mental Floss June 2022, mentalfloss.com/article/64451/11-delightful-icelandic-words-and-phrases

Van Biljon, Taylor, "10 Drops of Icelandic Wisdom: Some of our favorite Icelandic sayings." Buuble 2018, buubble.com/icelandic-sayings/

Wilde, Oscar, 1854-1900, *The Picture of Dorian Gray*, London UK; New York, N.Y.; Penguin, 2003.

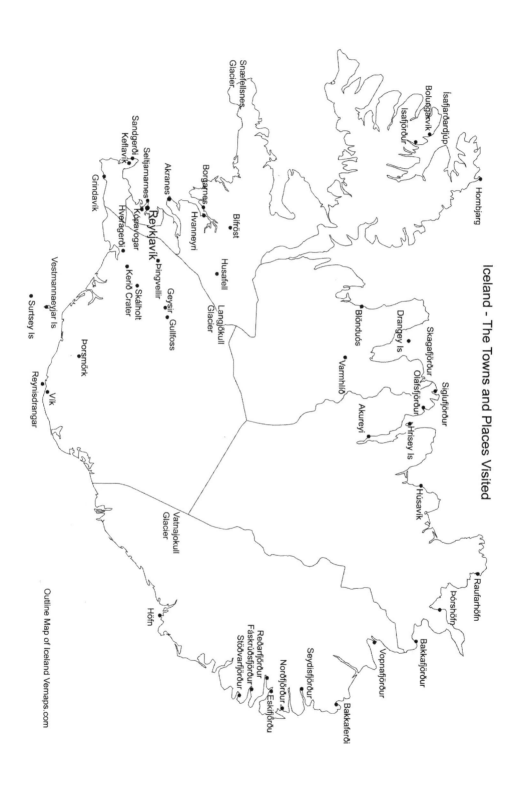

Iceland - The Towns and Places Visited

Outline Map of Iceland Vemaps.com

Hornbjarg

Ísafjarðardjúp
Bolungavík
Ísafjörður

Snæfellsnes
Glacier

Sandgerði
Keflavík

Grindavík

Seltjarnarnes
Akranes
Borgarnes
Hvanneyri

Reykjavík
Kópavogur
Hveragerði
Þingvellir
Kerið Crater
Skálholt
Geysir
Gullfoss

Bifröst

Húsafell

Langjökull
Glacier

Blönduós

Drangey Is

Skagafjörður
Ólafsfjörður
Siglufjörður

Varmahlíð

Akureyi
Hrísey Is

Húsavík

Vestmannaeyjar Is

Surtsey Is

Þorsmörk

Vík

Reynisdrangar

Vatnajökull
Glacier

Höfn

Raufarhöfn
Þórshöfn

Bakkafjörður

Vopnafjörður

Seyðisfjörður

Reðarfjörður
Fáskrúðsfjörður
Norðfjörður
Eskifjörðu
Stöðvarfjörður

Bakkaferði

Made in the USA
Middletown, DE
11 October 2022

12392537R00151